Contents

International Buddhist Directory

Wisdom Publications London

First published in 1985
Wisdom Publications, 23 Dering Street,
London W1, England

© Wisdom Publications 1985

ISBN 0 86171 025 8

Set in Times by Characters of
Chard, Somerset and printed and
bound in Hong Kong by J. Helen
Productions.

Introduction

This, our first international Buddhist directory, reflects the huge growth in interest and activity in Buddhism throughout the world today. Twenty-five years ago it would have been difficult to find Buddhist centres outside the East. Now, as well as nineteen Asian countries, forty-four countries in Western and Eastern Europe, North and South America, the Middle East, Africa and Australia and New Zealand are represented here.

Altogether, this directory lists some 1800 Buddhist centres in sixty-three counries. The first 500 – *Part One: Confirmed Addresses* – give information, confirmed as correct at the end of 1984, about the name, address, phone number, which tradition of Buddhism, the spiritual director, whether the centre is in the city of country, or has a resident teacher, accommodation, regular teachings, meditation and retreat facilities, library, bookshop, and newletter. The information in *Part Two: Unconfirmed Addresses*, which lists some 1300 names and addresses, was gleaned from various sources and has not been confirmed by the centres in question.

The information here is not definitive, but it is a start. We hope that centres and individuals will respond to this directory by updating and correcting what is printed here as well as supplying us with new information.

The only category of Buddhist activity in this directory is *Centres*. We want to expand future editions to include as many categories as possible of activities either directly Buddhist or connected with or supporting Buddhist activities. For example: artists, bookshops, computer services, filmmakers, food shops, journals, libraries, magazines, newspapers, restaurants, printers, publishers, schools, typesetters – these and more could be included.

We would like to thank everyone who has participated in preparing this directory, especially Jock Noble for his work while in India with the Tushita Mahayana Meditation Centre.

Wisdom Publications
London, April 1985

Part One
Confirmed Addresses

NAME & ADDRESS	TELEPHONE	TRADITION/ AFFILIATION	SPIRITUAL HEAD	Resident Teacher	City Centre	Country Centre	Regular Teachings	Meditation Facilities	Organized Retreats	Accom-modation	Library	Bookshop	Newsletter
ARGENTINA													
Kagyu Tekchen Chöling, Esmeralda 1385 19E, Buenos Aires 1007	(392) 0043	Tibetan: Karma Kagyu	Kalou Rinpoche & Lama Sherab Dordje		●		●	●				●	
AUSTRALIA *New South Wales*													
Marpa House, Sugarloaf, Dungog, NSW 2420	(049) 92 1893	Tibetan: Karma Kagyu	Lama Chime Rinpoche	●		●		●		●			
Phap Bao Pagoda, cnr Endensor & Bibby's Rds, Bonny Rigg, Sydney, NSW 2177			Thich Bao Lac (Table1)	●	●	●	●	●		●	●	●	●
Sydney Meditation Community 13 Rocklands Rd, Wollstonecraft, NSW 2065	(02) 436 3263	All traditions (FWBO)	Maha Sthavira Sangharakshita		●		●	●	●				
Tenzing Ling Meditation Retreat Centre, c/o Quaama Post Office, Quaama, NSW 2550	(0649) 38344	Mahayana	Zasep Tulku Rinpoche			●			●	●	●		
Vajrayana Institute, 1 Guthrie Avenue, Cremorne, Sydney, NSW 2098.	(02) 909 1330	Mahayana (FPMT)	Lama Yeshe & Zopa Rinpoche	●	●	●	●	●	●	●	●	●	●
Wat Buddha Dhamma, 10 Mile Hollow, Wiseman's Ferry, NSW 2255. *Resident lay community; earth buildings*	(043) 73 1193	Theravada	Phra Khantipalo	●			●	●	●	●	●	●	●

AUSTRALIA Queensland

NAME & ADDRESS	TELEPHONE	TRADITION/ AFFILIATION	SPIRITUAL HEAD	Resident Teacher	City Centre	Country Centre	Regular Teachings	Meditation Facilities	Organized Retreats	Accommodation	Library	Bookshop	Newsletter
Brisbane Zen Group, 10 Lomond Tce, East Brisbane, Qld 4169	(07) 379 5962	Zen (Los Angeles Center)	Hakuyu Taizan Maezumi Roshi		●			●	●		●		●
Brisbane Buddhist Vihara and Meditation Centre, 78 Hampstead Rd, Brisbane, Qld 4101	(07) 44 4035	Theravada			●		●	●			●		●
Buddhist Federation of Australia, PO Box 4, Spring Hill, Brisbane, Qld 4000. *Psychology & other w/shops*		All traditions		●	●	●	●	●		●	●	●	●
Buddhist Society of Queensland, c/o PO Box 4, Spring Hill, Brisbane, Qld 4000. *Psychology & other w/shops; social work*		Theravada		●			●	●			●		●
Chenrezig City Centre, 51 Enoggera Rd. Newmarket, Brisbane, Qld 4051. *Psychology & other w/shops*	(07) 356 9523	Mahayana (FPMT)	Lama Yeshe & Zopa Rinpoche		●		●	●	●		●		
Chenrezig Institute, Highlands Road, Eudlo. Qld 4554. *Psychology & other w/shops; dance & tai chi*	(071) 45 9047	Mahayana (FPMT)	Lama Yeshe & Zopa Rinpoche	●	●	●	●	●	●	●	●	●	●
Dhammadinna House, Buddhist Study & Research Centre, PO Box 4, Spring Hill, Brisbane, Qld 4000. *Counselling; psychology; community work; w/shops*		Early Buddhism	Klaas de Jong				●	●			●	●	●
Loden Compassion Mahayana Centre, 10 Lomond Tce, East Brisbane, Qld 4169	(07) 391 5723	Tibetan	Geshe Thubten Loden	●	●		●	●	●		●		●

NAME & ADDRESS	TELEPHONE	TRADITION/ AFFILIATION	SPIRITUAL HEAD	Resident Teacher	City Centre	Country Centre	Regular Teachings	Meditation Facilities	Organized Retreats	Accom-modation	Library	Bookshop	Newsletter
Soto Zen Buddhist Society, 33 Cairns Rd, Camira, Brisbane, Qld 4300. *Psychology, sacred dances, w/shops*	(07) 288 2413	Mahayana		•	•		•	•		•	•		
Vietnamese Buddhist Association of Queensland Inc, 48 Browne St, Corinda, Brisbane, Qld 4075	(07) 379 6007	Mahayana	Rev Thich Nhut Tan	•	•		•				•		
AUSTRALIA South Australia													
Buddha House, Centre for Advanced Buddhist Studies, PO Box 93, Eastwood, Adelaide, SA 5063	(08) 278 3970 (08) 277 8522	Mahayana (FPMT)	Lama Yeshe & Zopa Rinpoche	•	•		•	•	•		•	•	•
AUSTRALIA Tasmania													
Illusion Farm Retreat Centre, Lorinna, Tas 7306	(003) 63 5178	Mahayana	Zasep Tulku Rinpoche			•	•	•	•	•			•
AUSTRALIA Victoria													
Atisha Centre, Sandhurst Town Road RSD, Eaglehawk, Melbourne, Vic 3556. *Psychology & other w/shops; tai chi*	(054) 46 9033	Mahayana (FPMT)	Lama Yeshe & Zopa Rinpoche	•		•	•	•		•	•	•	•
Buddhist Society of Victoria, 226 Mary St, Richmond, Melbourne, Vic 3121.	(03) 428 2406	Theravada		•	•		•	•			•	•	•

NAME & ADDRESS	TELEPHONE	TRADITION/ AFFILIATION	SPIRITUAL HEAD	Resident Teacher	City Centre	Country Centre	Regular Teachings	Meditation Facilities	Organized Retreats	Accom- modation	Library	Bookshop	Newsletter
Buddhist Discussion Centre (Upwey) 33 Brooking St, Upwey, Vic 3158. *Chan & Thanka painting; teacher training*	(03) 754 3334	All traditions		●	●		●	●	●	●	●		●
Centre for Metaphysical Experience, 18 Foster Rd, Eltham, Vic 3095. *Psychology & other w/shops; children's classes; 7 day week counselling*	(03) 439 4493	Mahayana	Lama Yeshe	●	●		●	●				●	●
Melbourne University Buddhist Society, c/o Box 27, Union Bldg, Melbourne University, Grattan St, Parkville, Vic 3052		Mahayana		●			●				●		
Monash University Buddhist Society, Clayton, Vic 3168. *Shrine*	(03) 541 3144				●		●	●			●		●
Tara Institute, 3 Crimea St, St Kilda, Melbourne, Vic 3182. *Psychology & other w/shops*	(03) 51 3784. (03) 529 7704	Mahayana (FPMT)	Lama Yeshe & Zopa Rinpoche		●		●	●	●	●	●		●
Tibetan Buddhist Society, 178 George St, East Melbourne, Vic 3002.	(03) 417 3831	Tibetan: Gelug	Geshe Acharya Loden	●	●		●	●			●		●
AUSTRALIA Western Australia													
The Buddhist Centre (The Buddhist Society of WA Inc), 4 Magnolia St, North Perth, W.A 6006. *Dhamma school for children*	(09) 444 7013	Theravada		●	●	●	●	●	●	●		●	●
Loden Tharpa Choling Mahayana Centre 18 Union St, Subiaco, Perth, W.A 6008. *Visiting Lamas*	(09) 381 1405	Mahayana	Geshe Loden		●		●	●	●		●		

NAME & ADDRESS	TELEPHONE	TRADITION/ AFFILIATION	SPIRITUAL HEAD	Resident Teacher	City Centre	Country Centre	Regular Teachings	Meditation Facilities	Organized Retreats	Accommodation	Library	Bookshop	Newsletter
Origins Centre, 47 Bedford Ave, Subiaco, Perth, WA 6008	(09) 381 5535	Tibetan: Kagyu	Namgyal Rinpoche	●	●	●	●	●	●	●	●		●
AUSTRIA													
Bodhidharma Zendo, Fleischmarkt 16, 1010 Vienna	(222) 52 37 19	Zen	Rev Genro Koudela	●	●	●	●	●	●				●
Buddhistische Religionsgemeinschaft				●	●	●	●	●					●
Arya Maitreya Mandala, Postfach 61, 1051 Vienna. *Psychology & other w/shops*	(222) 436 68 64	Tibetan: Vajrayana	Lama Anagarika Govinda				●					●	
Buddhistisches Zentrum Schiebbs, Ginselberg 12, 3272 Scheibbs. *Psychology & other w/shops; dance; tai chi; art; healing*	(074) 82 24 12	All traditions					●	●	●	●	●	●	●
Jodo Shin Austria, Merianstr 29/4/52, 5020 Salzburg. *Social ethics*	(06222) 79 09 52	Amida: Jodo Shin	HH Zennon Rosho Othani (Japan)	●		●	●						●
Karma de Phel Ling, Gauitsch 56. 8442 Kitzeck		Tibetan: Vajrayana	HH Gyalwa Karmapa				●	●	●		●	●	
Tashi Rabten, Letzehof, 6800 Feldkirch.	(05522) 2 41 92	Tibetan	Geshe Rabten	●			●				●		
BANGLADESH													
Dhammarajika Buddhist Monastery, Kamalapur, Dacca 14.			Suddhananda Mahathero		●					●			

Name & Address	Telephone	Tradition/Affiliation	Spiritual Head	Resident Teacher	City Centre	Country Centre	Regular Teachings	Meditation Facilities	Organized Retreats	Accommodation	Library	Bookshop	Newsletter
BELGIUM													
Karma Sonam Gyamtso Ling Grote Hondstraat 36, 2018 Antwerp, Belgium.	(85) 21 48 20	Tibetan: Kagyu	Ven Kalu Rinpoche	●	●		●	●	●	●	●	●	●
Samyé Dzong – Karma Shedrup Gyamtso Ling, Rue Capouillet 33, 1060 Brussels. *Psychology & other w/shops; yoga; Tibetan language; art*	(02) 537 54 07	Tibetan: Kagyu	HH Gyalwa Karmapa	●	●		●	●	●	●	●	●	●
Yeunten Ling, Chateau de Fond L'Eveque, Promenade St Jean L'Agneau 4, 5201 Tihange-Huy. *Psychology & other w/shops; dance; tai chi; theatre; City Centre in Antwerp*	(03) (85) 21 48 20	Tibetan: Kagyu	Kalu Rinpoche			●							
BRAZIL													
Reiyukai do Brasil, 01531 Av Aclimacão 691, Saó Paulo	(011) 278 2056 & 278 2816	Mahayana	Tsugunari Kubo		●		●	●	●				
CANADA *Alberta*													
Edmonton Dharmadhatu, Apt 301, 10442 82 Avenue, Edmonton T6E 2A2	(403) 432 1788	Tibetan: Kagyu	Chogyam Trungpa Rinpoche		●		●	●	●		●		●

NAME & ADDRESS	TELEPHONE	TRADITION/AFFILIATION	SPIRITUAL HEAD	Resident Teacher	City Centre	Country Centre	Regular Teachings	Meditation Facilities	Organized Retreats	Accommodation	Library	Bookshop	Newsletter
CANADA *British Columbia*													
'Buddha's World', The Reijukai Society of BC, Suite 304, 1236 West 11th Ave, Vancouver, V6H 1K5	(604) 733 6737	Mahayana	Tsugunari Kubo	•		•	•	•		•	•	•	•
Thubten Kunga Choling, Victoria Buddhist Dharma Society, 1149 Leonard St, Victoria V8V 2S3. *Counselling*	(604) 385 4828	Tibetan: Sakya	HH Sakya Trizin	•	•		•	•			•		
Victoria Dharma Study Group, 608 Toronto St, Victoria V8V 1PG	(604) 385 7562	Tibetan: Kagyu	Chogyam Trungpa Rinpoche	•	•		•	•					
Victoria Zen Centre, 203 Goward Rd, Victoria V8X 3X3		Zen			•			•					
Zen Centre of Vancouver, 4985 Moss St, Vancouver V5R 3T5	(604) 433 4052	Zen			•			•	•				•
CANADA *Ontario*													
Dharmadhatu, 555 Bloor St West, Toronto, M5S 1Y6. *Psychology & other w/shops; Shambhala trg; Dharma art activities*	(416) 535 5882	Tibetan: Vajrayana	Chogyam Trungpa Rinpoche	•	•		•	•			•	•	•
Dharma Centre of Canada, PO Box 5549, Station 'A', Toronto M5W 1N7. *Psychology & other w/shops*		Tibetan: Vajrayana	Namgyal Rinpoche	•	•		•	•			•	•	•
Dharma Study Group, 129½ Hunter St West, Peterborough K9H ZK7	(705) 748 6571	Tibetan: Kagyu	Chogyam Trungpa Rinpoche		•		•	•			•	•	

NAME & ADDRESS	TELEPHONE	TRADITION/ AFFILIATION	SPIRITUAL HEAD	Newsletter	Bookshop	Library	Accommodation	Organized Retreats	Meditation Facilities	Regular Teachings	Country Centre	City Centre	Resident Teacher
Gaden Choling Mahayana Buddhist Meditation Centre, 114 Marchmount Rd, Toronto MG6 2B1. *Psychology & other w/shops; dance; tai chi*	(416) 651 3849	Tibetan: Gelug	HH Ling Rinpoche	●	●	●	●	●	●	●		●	●
Karma Tilo Chompheling, The Milachokor Karmapa Foundation, 834 Windermere Ave, Toronto M65 3M6. *Psychology & other w/shops; dance; tai chi*	(416) 767 4513	Tibetan: Kagyu	HH Gyalwa Karmapa & Karma Thinley Rinpoche	●	●	●	●	●	●	●	●	●	●
Zen Buddhist Temple, 46 Gwynne Ave, Toronto M6K 2C3	(416) 533 6911	Zen: Korean	Samu Sunim			●			●	●		●	●
CANADA Quebec													
Dharmadhatu, 5311 Ave du Parc, Suite 200, Montreal H2V 4G9	(514) 279 9115	Tibetan: Kagyu	Chogyam Trungpa Rinpoche	●		●	●	●	●	●		●	●
Milarepa Dharma Centre/Kagyu Rimay Chuday, 224 Old Settler's Rd, Box 53, Montreal JOR IHO	(514) 226 3174	Tibetan: Kagyu	HH Gyalwa Karmapa, H E Shamar & Kalu Rinpoche			●		●	●	●	●		
Temple Bouddhiste Tibetain, 1589 Vercheres Str, Longueuil, Montreal J4K 2Z6	(514) 679 5543	Tibetan	Geshe Kenrabt Gajam	●				●	●	●		●	●
CHILE													
Dharma Study Group, Pocuro 3049. Dep 11 Santiago	223 8959	Tibetan: Kagyu	Chogyam Trungpa Rinpoche					●		●		●	●

NAME & ADDRESS	TELEPHONE	TRADITION/ AFFILIATION	SPIRITUAL HEAD	Resident Teacher	City Centre	Country Centre	Regular Teachings	Meditation Facilities	Organized Retreats	Accommodation	Library	Bookshop	Newsletter
Karma Chile Thegsum Chöling, Conj El Libano, Psje Dos 5150, Macul, Santiago 11		Tibetan: Karma Kagyu	Lama Tounsang					•			•	•	
DENMARK													
Karma Drub DJY Ling, Centre of Tibetan Buddhist Studies, Svanemollevej 56, 2100 Copenhagen. *Picture sales: Lamas, old & new Thankas*	(01) 29 27 11	Tibetan	HH Gyalwa Karmapa	•	•		•	•		•		•	•
Karma Nalanda Buddhist – Christian Peace Centre, Hesbjergvej 50, 5491 Blommenslyst. *Dance & tai chi; peace research, agriculture, arts*	(09) 96 75 05	Tibetan & Theravada	HH The Dalai Lama			•	•	•			•	•	
FINLAND													
Helsingen Buddhalainen Keskus, PL 288, SF-00121, Helsinki 12	64 24 62	All traditions (FWBO)	Maha Sthavira Sangharakshita	•	•		•	•	•		•	•	•
FRANCE													
Centres D'Etudes Bouddhiques, 16 rue Thiers, 38000 Grenoble. *Dance & tai chi*	(76) 46 73 71	All traditions		•	•		•	•	•			•	•

NAME & ADDRESS	TELEPHONE	TRADITION/ AFFILIATION	SPIRITUAL HEAD	Resident Teacher	City Centre	Country Centre	Regular Teachings	Meditation Facilities	Organized Retreats	Accommodation	Library	Bookshop	Newsletter
Dorje Pamo Monastery, Chateau d'En Clausade, Marzens, 81500 Lavaur. *Community of Western nuns*	(63) 41 44 22	Mahayana (FPMT)	Lama Yeshe & Zopa Rinpoche	•		•	•	•	•		•	•	•
Institut Kagyu Vajradhara Ling, Domaine du Chateau d'Osmont, Aubry le Panthou, 61120 Vimoutiers. *Psychology & other w/shops; dance & tai chi; yoga; astrology*	(33) 39 00 44	Tibetan: Karma Kagyu	Khempo Kalu Rinpoche	•		•	•	•	•		•	•	•
Institut Vajra Yogini, Chateau d'En Clausade, Marzens, 81500 Lavaur. *Psychology & other w/shops; dance & tai chi*	(63) 58 17 22	Mahayana (FPMT)	Lama Yeshe & Zopa Rinpoche	•		•	•	•	•		•	•	•
Kagyu Chedroup Tcheuling, Boulevard Malou, Ave du General Leclerc, Allauch 13190. *Tibetan language*	(16-91) 68 24 19	Tibetan: Kagyu	Kalu Rinpoche		•		•	•			•	•	•
Kagyu Ling, La Boulaye, 71320 Toulon sur Arroux.	(85) 79 43 41	Tibetan: Kagyu	Kalu Rinpoche			•	•				•	•	
Karma Gyurme Ling, Druk Dechen Ling, 27 Rte de Rosheim, 67530 Boersch	(88) 95 87 84	Tibetan:	HH Gyalwa Karmapa & H E Kyabje Thykse Rinpoche	•		•	•	•	•	•		•	•
Karma Ling, Abbey St Hugon, 73110 Arvillard. *Psychology & other w/shops; yoga*	(79) 65 64 62	Tibetan: Kagyu	Kalu Rinpoche	•		•	•	•		•	•	•	
Karma Migyur Ling, Montchardon Izeron, St Marcellin, 38160 Isere. *Yoga*	(76) 38 33 13	Tibetan: Kagyu	HH Gyalwa Karmapa	•		•	•	•	•		•	•	

NAME & ADDRESS	TELEPHONE	TRADITION/ AFFILIATION	SPIRITUAL HEAD	Resident Teacher	City Centre	Country Centre	Regular Teachings	Meditation Facilities	Organized Retreats	Accommodation	Library	Bookshop	Newsletter
Le Voyage Intérieur, 54 Boulevard Meusnier de Querlon, 44000 Nantes	(40) 59 18 17	Mahayana	Tsugunari Kubo	•	•		•	•	•		•		
Nalanda Monastery, Rouzegas, Labastide St Georges, 81500 Lavaur *Community of Western monks*	(63) 58 02 25	Mahayana (FPMT)	Lama Yeshe & Zopa Rinpoche	•		•	•	•					
Paris Dharma Study Group, c/o Karr, 2 Square du Roule, 75008 Paris	562 38 89	Tibetan: Kagyu	Chogyam Trungpa Rinpoche	•			•	•	•		•	•	•
Rigpa, 11 Rue Denis Poisson, 75017 Paris	572 51 34	Tibetan: Nyingma	Sogyal Rinpoche				•	•					
GERMANY													
Aryatara Institut, Jägerndorf 1½, 8382 Arnstorf. *Movement & other w/shops*	(08723) 2396	Mahayana (FPMT)	Lama Yeshe & Zopa Rinpoche	•			•	•	•	•	•	•	•
Buddhist Association Hannover, Bünteweg 50, 3000 Hannover 71	(0511) 52 04 29	All traditions						•			•	•	•
Buddhistische Gemeinschaft Jodo Shinshu, Courbierestr 8, 1000 Berlin 30	(030) 211 91 13	Shin-Buddhism	Monshu Koshin Ohtani					•			•	•	•
Buddhistischer Tempel, Rubinstr 14, 8000 München 50	(089) 150 41 88	Tibetan	HH The Dalai Lama		•	•							
Dharma Study Group Marburg, Zwetschenweg 23, 3550 Marburg	(06421) 29 20 94	Tibetan: Kagyu (FWBO)	Chogyam Trungpa Rinpoche	•	•		•	•	•		•		
FWBO Germany, Rechstr 9 43 Essen 11			Maha Sthavira Sangharakshita	•	•		•	•	•		•	•	•

Karuna Refuge

Karuna Refuge is a place of retreat. It offers the opportunity to live a more quiet and contemplative life on secluded pastoral land near the village of Molyvos (classical Mithimna) on the Greek isle of Lesvos.

Karuna is ideally situated in a sheltered enclave amidst the sun-dazzled, rugged terrain of the Aegean islands.

The tranquil beauty, unspoilt peace of the surrounding countryside and temperate Mediterranean climate provide the right environment for a balanced development of mind and body.

Karuna welcomes all people who need to do retreat in a peaceful and beautiful environment and who have a deep felt, genuine desire for psychological well-being.

Small groups of no more than 20 people can be catered for.

Karuna caters for disciplines both East and West, as well as intensive courses on meditation, religion, psychology, physiotherapy, art and the like.

For more information contact Yorgo Cassapidis, Karuna Refuge, Molyvos, Isle of Lesvos, Greece. Tel: (0253) 71486.

NAME & ADDRESS	TELEPHONE	TRADITION/ AFFILIATION	SPIRITUAL HEAD	Resident Teacher	City Centre	Country Centre	Regular Teachings	Meditation Facilities	Organized Retreats	Accommodation	Library	Bookshop	Newsletter
Haus der Stille, Mühlenweg 20, 2059 Roseburg üb Büchen. *Psychology & other w/shops*	(04158) 214	Tibetan, Zen, Theravada				●		●	●	●	●	●	●
Kagyu Shjen Phen Kyn Thjab, c/o Katola Becker, Schulplatz 12, 4133 Neukirchen-Vluyn	(0203) 35 9878	Tibetan: Kagyu	HH Gyalwa Karmapa			●	●	●			●	●	
Karma Tashi Ling, Am Dausenel-busch 16, 5600 Wuppertal, North Rhine Westfalia. *Dance; tai chi & shiatsu*	(0202) 59 0323	Tibetan: Karma Kagyu	HH Gyalwa Karmapa				●	●			●	●	
Karma Lodrö Ling, Im Rotenbach 2, 7449 Neckartenzlingen		Tibetan: Karma Kagyu	HH Gyalwa Karmapa		●	●	●	●	●		●		●
Manjushri Mandala School for Spiritual Astro Energetics, Hausnummer 50, 8651 Grafengehaig. *Psychology & other w/shops; astrology*	(09255) 1747	All traditions	Tenga Rinpoche					●			●		
Samye Dzong Berlin, c/o U Küstner, Kalckreuthstr 14, 1000 Berlin 30. *Weekly mtgs*	(030) 211 75 71 or 784 56 06	Tibetan: Karma Kagyu	Akong Rinpoche		●			●			●		
Tibetisches Zentrum Hamburg e.V. Hermann Balkstr 106, 2000 Hamburg 73. *Tibetan language*	(040) 644 35 85	Tibetan: Gelug	HH Dalai Lama Geshe Rabten	●	●		●	●	●	●	●	●	●
GREECE													
Karuna Refuge Meditation Retreat Centre, Mithimna (Molyvos), Isle of Lesbos GR 881 08	(0252) 71 486	Independent				●		●	●	●	●	●	

NAME & ADDRESS	TELEPHONE	TRADITION/ AFFILIATION	SPIRITUAL HEAD	Resident Teacher	City Centre	Country Centre	Regular Teachings	Meditation Facilities	Organized Retreats	Accommodation	Library	Bookshop	Newsletter
HOLLAND													
Buddhayana Centre, Fronemanstr 16B, The Hague, 2572 VG. *Psychology & other w/shops: regular mtgs*	(0) 70 46 52 94	Theravada	Dharmawiranatha	•	•		•		•		•	•	•
FWBO Netherlands, Vrijenbansestr 25b, 3037 VV Rotterdam		All traditions (FWBO)	Maha Sthavira Sangharakshita	•			•					•	
Maitreya Institut, Raadhuisdyk 9, 6627 AC Maasbommel. *Psychology & other w/shops; slide shows; teaching facilities: 3 monthly magazine*	(08876) 2188	Mahayana (FPMT)	Lama Yeshe & Zopa Rinpoche	•			•		•	•	•	•	•
Meditation Centre 'De Kosmos', Prins Hendrikkade 142. Amsterdam. *Psychology & other w/shops; tai chi; dance; yoga; esoterics & health*		All traditions			•			•			•		•
Stichting Vrienden van het Boeddhisme, Eperweg 49 – 18. 8072 DA Nunspeet	(03412) 54120	All traditions	Prof R H C Janssen			•	•	•	•	•	•		•
Vipasana International Meditation Centre, (contact address: Lisserweg 487a, Lisserbroek 2165 AS). Centre is in Igatpuri, India.		Vipasana	S N Goenka										•
HONG KONG													
Dharma Group, 1501 Cambridge House, 26-28 Cameron Rd, Tsim Sha Tsui. *Weekly mtgs*	(3) 721974	Mahayana (FPMT)	Lama Yeshe & Zopa Rinpoche				•	•				•	

NAME & ADDRESS	TELEPHONE	TRADITION/ AFFILIATION	SPIRITUAL HEAD	Resident Teacher	City Centre	Country Centre	Regular Teachings	Meditation Facilities	Organized Retreats	Accommodation	Library	Bookshop	Newsletter
Vajrayana Esoteric Society (Dudjom Ashram), Flat A, 6/F, 692–702 King's Rd, North Point. *Psychology & other w/shops*	(5) 619811	Tibetan: Vajrayana	HH Dudjom Rinpoche	•	•		•	•			•	•	•
The World Fellowship of Buddhists, Hong Kong & Macau Regional Centre, Lucky Mansion, 14/F, Block GH, Jordan Rd, Kowloon	(3) 660572	Non-sectarian	Yen Why & Upaska P Y Ko			•	•	•			•		•
HUNGARY													
Buddhist Mission/East European Center of the Arya Maitreya Mandala, Muzeu Str 5, Budapest 1088	130 169	Tibetan: Vajrayana	Lama Anagarika Govinda	•	•	•	•	•			•	•	•
INDIA													
All Assam Buddhist Assocn, Desangpani Buddhist Temple, PO Desangpani, Sibsagar, Assam		Theravada	Aniruddha Bhikku	•		•	•	•	•	•	•	•	•
Bir Sakya Lama's School, PO Chowgan, Via Bir, Dist Mandi, Himachal Pradesh		Tibetan: Vajrayana	HH The Sakya Trizin				•						
Bokard Buddha Vihara, Bokard Steel City, Dist Dhanbad, Bihar			Tsugunari Kubo	•		•				•	•		
Buddha Vihara, Mandir Marg New Delhi 110001	343328	Theravada	Ariyawabsa Nayaka Thsa	•	•			•			•	•	

NAME & ADDRESS	TELEPHONE	TRADITION/ AFFILIATION	SPIRITUAL HEAD	Resident Teacher	City Centre	Country Centre	Regular Teachings	Meditation Facilities	Organized Retreats	Accommodation	Library	Bookshop	Newsletter
Buddhist Education Institute, Buddhist House, Shyampurittapur, Dist Ghaziabad, Uttar Pradesh		Theravada					•		•			•	
The Buddhist International Centre, 160/4456 Pantnagar, Ghatkopar, Bombay 400075. *Seminars*		Theravada & Mahayana			•	•							•
Choling Monastery, PO Chowgan, Bir, Dist Mandi, Himachal Pradesh		Tibetan: Vajrayana/ Nyingma Tibetan	HH Dudjom Rinpoche										
International Buddha Child Welfare Centre Clement Town, Dehra Dun, Uttar Pradesh. *Psychology & other w/shops, orphan care*				•				•	•	•	•		
International Buddha Education Institute, Buddhalok, Meerut Rd, Hapur, Uttar Pradesh. *Psychology & other w/shops; orphan care*	2069	Theravada & Mahayana		•	•		•	•	•	•	•	•	•
Kalimpong Dharmodaya Sabha, 9¼ Mile, PO Kalimpong Dist, Darjeeling, West Bengal *Nursery school*		Theravada & Mahayana	Bhikkhu Shanta Rakkhita	•			•				•		
Ladakh Buddhist Assocn, New Gompa, Leh, Ladakh, Kashmir.	141 & 107	Tibetan											
Lamdon Social Welfare Society, PO Box 1, Leh, Ladakh, Jammu & Kashmir 194101		Tibetan											
Maha Bodhi Ashoka Mission, Dhamma Kuti, Buddha Vihara, Siddharth Marg, Mayo Link Rd, Ajmer, Rajasthan. *Psychology & other w/shops*	Applied for	Theravada	Rahula Suman Chawara & Lama Kushok Bakula Rinpoche	•			•	•		•		•	•

NAME & ADDRESS	TELEPHONE	TRADITION/ AFFILIATION	SPIRITUAL HEAD	Resident Teacher	City Centre	Country Centre	Regular Teachings	Meditation Facilities	Organized Retreats	Accom-modation	Library	Bookshop	Newsletter
Mass Movement (Buddhist Brotherhood), 51 Siddharth Vihar, Wadala, Bombay, Maharashtra 400031. *Psychology & other w/shops*	882 3678	Mahayana & Theravada	Dhammachari Lok-mitra	●	●		●	●	●	●	●	●	●
Mass Movement (Buddhist Brotherhood), Ambedkar Nagar, P L Lokhande Marg, Pestamsagar, Chembur, Maharashtra, Bombay 400089			Sangharatna	●	●		●	●	●	●	●		
Nagarjuna Buddhist Foundation, (Research Centre), 18 Andhiari Bagh, Gorakhpur, Uttar Pradesh 273001, *Academic lectures & publication of; seminars, books & research*	3258										●	●	
Nipponzan Myohoji, c/o Venu-van-Vihar, PO Rajgir, Nalanda, Bihar 803116	30 32 62	Japanese Mahayana	Nichidatsu Fujii							●			
Nyingma Monastery, PO Chowgan, Bir Dist Mandi, Himachal Pradesh		Tibetan: Nyingma	HH Dudjom Rinpoche										
Pal Phuntsok Choe Khor Ling (Khampa Gar Monastery, Tashi Jong, PO Paprola, Dist Kangra, Himachal Pradesh 176115	Baijnath 47	Tibetan: Kagyu	HE Khamtul Rinpoche										
The Reiyukai, 168 Jor Bagh, Union Territory, New Delhi 110003	617594 & 694692	Mahayana	Tsugunari Kubo	●	●		●	●	●				
Reiyukai – Darjeeling, 8 Mehtab Chand Rd, Queen Hill, PO Darjeeling, West Bengal	3057		Tsugunari Kubo	●		●	●	●			●		
Reiyukai Darjeeling Office, 5DB Giri Rd, PO & Dist, Darjeeling, West Bengal 734101	3057		Tsugunari Kubo	●			●	●					

NAME & ADDRESS	TELEPHONE	TRADITION/ AFFILIATION	SPIRITUAL HEAD	Resident Teacher	City Centre	Country Centre	Regular Teachings	Meditation Facilities	Organized Retreats	Accommodation	Library	Bookshop	Newsletter
Sakya Centre, 187 Rajpur Rd, PO Rajpur Dehra Dun, Uttar Pradesh 248009. *Tibetan handicrafts – export*	(84) 286	Sakya	HH Sakya Trizin	●	●	●	●	●	●	●	●	●	
Sherabling Institute of Buddhist Studies, PO Sansal 176125, Dist Kangra, Himachal Pradesh.	HP 13	Tibetan: Kagyu (Kamtshang)	HE Tai Situ Rinpoche	●		●	●	●		●	●		
Tharpa Retreat Centre, Barlowganj, Dist Dehra Dun, Uttar Pradesh, 248122. *Lama Chopa group meetings: occasional teachings*		Tibetan: Gelug	Geshe Kelsang Gyatso							●			
Tibet House, 1 Institutional Area, Lodi Rd, New Delhi, 110003.	611515	Non sectarian	HH The Dalai				●				●	●	
Triratna Buddha Mission, PO Phulout, Dist Saharsa Bihar				●									
Tushita Mahayana Meditation Centre, 5/5 Shantiniketan, New Delhi 110021. *Psychology & other w/shops*	675468	Mahayana (FPMT)	Lama Yeshe & Zopa Rinpoche		●	●	●	●	●		●	●	
Tushita Retreat Centre, McLeod Ganj, Upper Dharamsala, Dist Kangra, Himachal Pradesh	Dharamsala 266	Mahayana (FPMT)	Lama Yeshe & Zopa Rinpoche			●	●	●	●	●	●	●	
Vishva Shanti, Phungyi Kyanng, Port Blair, Andamans 744101, Andaman & Nicobar Islands	2033	Burmese Buddhism	U Ginawonsa		●			●		●	●		●
INDONESIA													
Dhammadipa Arama, Ds Mojorejo, Kec. Batu, Malang		Theravada	Bhikkhu Khemasarano Thera	●			●	●		●		●	

NAME & ADDRESS	TELEPHONE	TRADITION/ AFFILIATION	SPIRITUAL HEAD	Resident Teacher	City Centre	Country Centre	Regular Teachings	Meditation Facilities	Organized Retreats	Accom-modation	Library	Bookshop	Newsletter
Romelan, Balapan Kemakmuran No 6A Yogyakarta. *Psychology & other w/shops; dance & tai chi* **Vihara Mendut**, Desa Mendut, Magelang, PO Box 7 Muntilan (Jateng)		Theravada	Pannavaro	•	•				•		•		
IRELAND *(Republic of)*													
Karma Dagpo Chukhor Ling, 11 North Trce, Inchicore, Dublin 8	(0001) 718491	Tibetan: Kagyu	Chuje Akong Rinpoche		•		•	•	•		•	•	•
Manjushri Mandala, Glenview House, Portsalon, Donegal. *Psychology & other w/shops; astrology*	(02533) 2599	All traditions	Tenga Rinpoche			•	•	•	•	•	•	•	
ITALY													
Associazione Buddhista Italiana, Via Fra Bartolomeo 49, 50124 Florence. *Studies & researches re Hinayana Buddhism; publication Buddhismo Scientifico*	(055) 57 39 91/ 22 68 88	Theravada											
Associazione Zen Italia, Via Baldinucci 1, 20158 Milan	(02) 608 62 62				•						•		
Centro Cenresig, Via Acri 2, 40100 Bologna	(051) 34 45 92	Mahayana (FPMT)	Lama Yeshe & Zopa Rinpoche		•			•			•	•	•

NAME & ADDRESS	TELEPHONE	TRADITION/ AFFILIATION	SPIRITUAL HEAD	Resident Teacher	City Centre	Country Centre	Regular Teachings	Meditation Facilities	Organized Retreats	Accommodation	Library	Bookshop	Newsletter
Centro Ciang Ciub Ling, Cascina Ratta, Frazione Perego, 22050 Como		Tibetan: Gelug	Ghesce Tenzin Gompo		●								
Centro di Cultura Buddhista, c/o Prof Riccardo Venturini, Via del Castro Pretorio 20, 00185 Rome													
Centro d'Informazione Buddhista, Via Pio Rolla 71, 10094 Giaveno, Torino. *Tibetan medicine & art; picture & music archives; Buddhist inconography courses; info on other European centres*	(011) 937 83 31	All traditions				●					●		
Centro Ghe Pel Ling, Viale Romolo 1, 3014 3 Milan. *3 yr courses philosophy & psychology; research on Buddhism in the West, conferences; AV material on Tibet; publications of Lamas' teachings*	(02) 837 51 08	Tibetan: Gelug	Ghesce Rabten	●	●		●	●					
Centro Italiano Zen Soto – Un Templo Buddhista, Via Gaetana Agnesi 18 20135 Milano	(02) 546 21 49	Zen Soto		●	●		●	●	●				
Centro Lama Tzong Khapa, Piazza Vittorio Emmanuele 18, 31050 Villorba, Treviso. *Psychology*	(0422) 92 80 79	Mahayana (FPMT)	Lama Yeshe & Zopa Rinpoche			●	●	●	●	●		●	
Centro Maitri, Via Ormea 28/30C, 10125 Torino. *Psychology, yoga, mental trg courses*	(011) 59 30 97	Tibetan: Gelug	Ghesce Rabten Rinpoche		●		●	●					
Centro Milarepa, Via Saibante 3, 10064 Pinerolo Torino. *Guru Yoga of Milarepa: publications of Tibetan rites, texts etc.*	(0121) 2 24 84	Tibetan: Kagyu	Lama Gian Ciup	●		●	●	●	●			●	

NAME & ADDRESS	TELEPHONE	TRADITION/ AFFILIATION	SPIRITUAL HEAD	Resident Teacher	City Centre	Country Centre	Regular Teachings	Meditation Facilities	Organized Retreats	Accommodation	Library	Bookshop	Newsletter
Centro Samanthabadra, Via Capo Palinuro 34, 00050, Ostia, Rome.	(06) 503 72 52	Tibetan: Gelug				•		•		•			
Centro Tekciok Samling, Via Donadei 8, 12060 Belvedere Langhe, Cuneo. *Hatha Yoga: tai chi; Buddhism courses*	(011) 959 37 80 (0173) 79632	Tibetan; Gelug	Ghesce Ciampa Lodro					•		•			
Centro Zen, Corso Cavallotti 21, 28100 Novara. *Sesshin: tai chi; Pa-Twan-Chi. Reserve accomdn*	(0321) 20121	Zen Rinzai	Engaku Taine										
Centro Zen Rinzai, c/o Centro Macrobiotico, Via Don Bosco 18, 48018 Faenza		Zen Rinzai											
Centro Zen Rinzai Via Porcari 3, 00100 Rome													
Centro Zen Rinzai, c/o Leo Alfonsi, Via Corticella 216/7, 40128 Bologna		Zen Rinzai											
Centro Zen Soto, c/o Palestra Yamato Fiamma, Via Pinerolo 19, 00100 Rome		Zen Soto											
Centro Zen Soto, c/o Aldo Tollini, Via Don Sturzo 49/14, 30170 Venezia-Mestre		Zen Soto											
Comunita' Dzog-Chen, Dorje Tibetano, Corso Garibaldi 55, 20100 Milan	(02) 86 76 94	Tibetan: Dzog-Chen	Lama Namkhai Norbu Rinpoche										
Comunita Dzog-Chen – Merigar, Archidosso (Grosseto) 58031. *Yantra yoga, Tibetan Medicine, Tibetan astrology*		Tibetan Dzog-Chen	Lama Namkhai Norbu Rinpoche			•		•	•		•	•	•
Dojo Soto Zen, Via Saluzzo 23/A, 10125 Torino	(02) 60 86 62	Zen	Mjo Sho Lin Getsu										
Dojo Zen, Via Baldinucci 1, 20158 Milan. *Mtgs & conferences; publications Zen texts with comments of Master Taisen Deshimaru Roshi*		Soto Zen	Roberto Pinciara		•			•					

Correspondence Courses in Buddhist Studies

Lama Tzong Khapa Institute
A Buddhist residential and teaching centre in the Tuscan hills near Pisa, Italy, Lama Tzong Khapa Institute offers two major education programmes of complete Buddhist studies.

The Institute is a member of the Foundation for the Preservation of the Mahayana Tradition, a network of over 50 Buddhist teaching and meditation centres and other activities worldwide.

Education Programme
The Institute's longer programme for the *Geshe Degree* is adapted from similar Tibetan monastic training programmes. The second new course is the shorter *Master's Degree in Buddhist Philosophy and Meditation* and includes both sutra and tantra.

Because of the growing interest, the Institute is offering the first four courses of the Master's programme by correspondence.

Course 1 *Collected Topics*
An introduction to Buddhist philosophical analysis and worldview. 41 lectures on 20 tapes. £100/$150

Course 2 *Mind and Cognition*
An introduction to Buddhist psychology and epistemology. How we know and experience the world. 32 lectures on 16 tapes. £100/£150

Course 3 *Ways of Reasoning*
A more detailed study of logical forms of argument as taught by the Prasangika-Madhyamika system. An understanding of inferential logic as a means to a deeper, intuitive realization. 40 lectures on 20 tapes £100/$150

Course 4 *The Ornament for Clear Realizations*
This details and clarifies teachings of the Buddha on the role of the bodhisattva, a person committed to enlightenment. 160 lectures on 80 tapes. £400/$560

How to Order
Course fees include written material, review, examination and access to teaching staff.

For further details contact George Churinoff, Lama Tzong Khapa Institute, 56040 Pomaia, Italy. Telephone (050) 68976.

NAME & ADDRESS	TELEPHONE	TRADITION/ AFFILIATION	SPIRITUAL HEAD	Resident Teacher	City Centre	Country Centre	Regular Teachings	Meditation Facilities	Organized Retreats	Accommodation	Library	Bookshop	Newsletter
Dorje – Centro Raccolta e Documentazione Iconografica del Pantheon Lamaista, Trucco S Luigi 50, 10094 Giaveno, Torino. *Founded by painter Alessandri to reconstruct Lamaistic Tibetan pantheon*	(011) 937 64 39										●	●	●
Gruppo Zen Rinzai, c/o Toniatti Andrea, Melta di Gardolo 1, 38100 Trento		Zen											
Istituto Lama Tzong Khapa, 56040 Pomaia, Pisa. *Psychology; philosophy; hatha yoga, tai chi, Tibetan medicine; text translations: Buddhist correspondence courses*	(050) 68976 & 68894	Mahayana (FPMT)	Lama Yeshe & Zopa Rinpoche	●		●	●	●	●	●			
Istituto Samantabhadra, Via Adolfo Rava 30, 00142 Rome	540 90 36 & 503 72 52	Tibetan: Gelug			●			●		●			
Inner Trip Italia, Via Tonale 22, 20125 Milan	(02) 68 02 20		Tsugunari Kubo	●	●		●	●	●				
Karma Thegsum Tashi Ling, Contrada Morago 6, 37030 Mizzole-Cancello, Verona. *Cenresig Puja every Friday; camping is allowed*	(045) 39431	Tibetan	Tenga Rinpoche	●		●	●	●	●	●			
Lamaco, Libera Accademia di Meditazione e Arti Curative Orientali, Via Valgiombove 36, 06073 Corciano, Perugia. *Ayurvedic & Tibetan medicine courses; herborization stages; etc; publication Review Lamaco*		Tibetan: Sakya	nGan dZong Tonpa	●		●	●	●		●			

NAME & ADDRESS	TELEPHONE	TRADITION/ AFFILIATION	SPIRITUAL HEAD	Resident Teacher	City Centre	Country Centre	Regular Teachings	Meditation Facilities	Organized Retreats	Accom- modation	Library	Bookshop	Newsletter
Monastero Zen di Scaramuccia (Bukkosan Zenshin Ji), Franzione Bagni 126/R, 05019 Orvieto, Scalo. *Sesshin; climbing; skiing; tai chi; publication News of Scaramuccia (bi-monthly)*	(0763) 25054	Rinzai Zen	Engaku Taino	•		•							
Monastero Zen Soto, Via Gaetana Agnesi 18, 20135 Milan. *Sesshin; Zazenkai Sanzen; Samu; text explantns; Christian & Buddhist meditations*	(02) 546 21 49	Zen Soto	Bhiksu Ryusui Zen sen		•		•	•	•				
Pagoda Buddhista di Pieve a Socana, 52016 Castel Focognano, Arezzo. *May 1 to October 31 Pagoda let for retreats.*	(055) 57 39 91 & 22 68 88	Theravada		•		•				•	•		
Rigpa Centro di Meditazione Buddhista, Via Fornari, 4 – 20146 Milan **Zendo Rinzai**, c/o Centro Studi Yoga, Via Privata di Piazza Sanfront 21, 16043 Chiavari.	(02) 31 71 52	Tibetan: Nyingma	Lama Sogyal Rinpoche										
JAPAN													
Bukkyo Dendo Kyokai, (Buddhist Promoting Foundation), 3 – 14, Shiba – 4 Chome, Minato-ku, 108 Tokyo	03 455 58 51				•						•	•	
Reiyukai, 7-8 Azabudai, 1 Chome, Minato-ku, 106 Tokyo.	03 (585) 2501		Tsugunari Kubo	•	•		•	•	•		•	•	•
Tibet Culture Centre, 401 Gotanda Lila Hi-Town, 15-12-2 Nishi Gotanda, Shinagawa-Ku, Tokyo 141.	(03) 490 7868	Tibetan	HH Dalai Lama		•		•	•			•	•	•

NAME & ADDRESS	TELEPHONE	TRADITION/ AFFILIATION	SPIRITUAL HEAD	Resident Teacher	City Centre	Country Centre	Regular Teachings	Meditation Facilities	Organized Retreats	Accommodation	Library	Bookshop	Newsletter
KOREA													
Bul-II International Meditation Centre, Song Kwang Sa Monastery, Seung Ju Kun, 543-43 Cholla Namdo. *Facilities available only for monks and nuns.*	130 131 132	Korean Son Zen	Kusan Sunim	●	●	●	●	●	●	●	●		
MALAYSIA													
FWBO Malaysia, Lot 7, Taman Ria, Jln Salleh, Nujar, Johore		All traditions (FWBO) Non-sectarian	Maha Sthavira Sangharakshita	●	●		●	●	●		●	●	●
Jelutong Young Buddhist Society, 392 East Jelutong, Penang. *Tai chi; audio-visual library, children Sunday sch, dance.*	03 310234				●		●		●		●		
Klang & Coast Buddhist Association, 30 Jalan Raya Barat, Kelang, Selangor. *Free medical clinic*							●						
Malaysian Buddhist Association, 182 Burmah Road, Penang.	62655	Mahayana	Kim Beng, Amn	●	●		●			●	●	●	●
Pahang Buddhist Association Youth Group, D-187 Jalan Bukit Ubi, Kuantan, Pahang. *Buddhist cultural goods, Sunday Dharma Class*	095 28312	Mahayana	Sek Kim-Meng	●			●			●	●		
Sasana Abhiwurdhi Wardhana Society, Buddhist Vihara, 123 Jalan Berhaca, Brickfields, 09-06 Kuala Lumpur. *Psychology & other w/shops*	03-44 11 41	Theravada	K. Sri Dhammananda Maha Nayaka Thera	●	●		●	●			●		●

NAME & ADDRESS	TELEPHONE	TRADITION/ AFFILIATION	SPIRITUAL HEAD	Resident Teacher	City Centre	Country Centre	Regular Teachings	Meditation Facilities	Organized Retreats	Accommodation	Library	Bookshop	Newsletter
Seck Kia Eenh Dhamma School, 57 Jalan Gajah Berang, Melaka. *Dance; games; training & work camps.*	06-228210	Theravada	Kotawage Khemarama	●			●		●		●	●	●
Young Buddhist Association of Malaysia 38 Dickens Street, Penang. *Dance; tai chi; vegetarian resturant; youth counselling & activities, leadership training*	369591		K. Sri Dhammananda Maha Nayaka Thera & Chuk Mor & Kim Beng		●	●	●	●	●		●	●	●
MEXICO													
El Reiyukai, Reiyukai de Mexico AC, Ciencias 22, Col Escandon, Mexico DF 11800. contact Miguel Hidalgo	(515) 26 35	Reiyukai	Tsugunari Kubo	●	●		●	●					
MONGOLIA													
Gangdantekchenling Monastery, Gangdan, Ulan-Bator	29450	Mahayana	Khamb Lama Kh. Gaadan			●	●			●	●		●
NEPAL													
Himalayan Yogic Institute, Lazimpath, Kathmandu; GPO Box 817, Kathmandu		Mahayana (FPMT)	Lama Yeshe & Zopa Rinpoche		●		●	●	●		●	●	●
Kopan Mahayana Buddhist Centre, GPO Box 817, Kathmandu.		Mahayana (FPMT)	Lama Yeshe & Zopa Rinpoche	●		●	●	●	●	●	●	●	●

NAME & ADDRESS	TELEPHONE	TRADITION/ AFFILIATION	SPIRITUAL HEAD	Resident Teacher	City Centre	Country Centre	Regular Teachings	Meditation Facilities	Organized Retreats	Accom-modation	Library	Bookshop	Newsletter
Lawudo Retreat Centre, Thami Valley, GPO Box 817, Kathmandu		Mahayana (FPMT)	Lama Yeshe & Zopa Rinpoche			●		●	●	●		●	
Manimandapa Vihar, Dhapaga Bahil, Patako, Lalitpur 16.		Theravada	Bhikkhu Jyana purnika		●	●	●	●	●				
The Reiyukai, Nepal, 'Peace', Nepalese Reiyukai Office, PO Box 2136, Dhobhidhara Dilli. Bazar, Kathmandu	216615		Tsugunari Kubo	●	●	●	●	●	●		●	●	
Vipassana Meditation Centre, Buddha Vihara, Siddhartha Marg, PO Box 993, Kathmandu.	15743	Theravada	Bhikkhu Sumangala		●		●	●	●				
NEW ZEALAND													
Auckland Buddhist Centre, PO Box 68-453, Newton, Auckland. *Dance; tai chi; yoga.*	73 5604 & 77 1967	Western (FWBO)	Maha Sthavira Sangharakshita	●	●		●	●	●		●		●
Denkyo-Ji, 872 West Coast Rd., Oratia, Auckland.		Zen	Tekio Radford		●					●			
Dorje Chang Institute, Box 2814, 14 Carrick Place, Mount Eden, Auckland	60 0442	Mahayana (FPMT)	Lama Yeshe & Zopa Rinpoche	●			●	●	●			●	●
Karma Kagyu Thigsum Chokhorling, Boddhisattva Road, RD1 Kaukapakapa.	KPA 5428	Tibetan: Kagyu	HH The Karmapa			●		●				●	●
Mahamudra Centre for Universal Unity, Colville RD, Coromandel.	Colville 851	Mahayana (FPMT)	Lama Yeshe & Zopa Rinpoche	●		●	●	●	●			●	●

NAME & ADDRESS	TELEPHONE	TRADITION/ AFFILIATION	SPIRITUAL HEAD	Resident Teacher	City Centre	Country Centre	Regular Teachings	Meditation Facilities	Organized Retreats	Accommodation	Library	Bookshop	Newsletter
Wellington Buddhist centre, PO Box 12311 Wellington North		All traditions	Maha Sthavira Sangharakshita	●	●		●	●	●		●	●	●
New Zealand Karma Thegsum Choling, c/o JR Wrigley, 34 Second Avenue, Whangarei.	81 266	Tibetan: Kagyu	Beru Chentse Rinpoche		●			●					
NORWAY													
Karma Tashi Ling Buddhist Centre, Meklenborgveien, Oslo 12. *Courses by visiting Lamas.*	(02) 29 15 49	Tibetan: Kagyu	HH Gyalwa Karmapa	●	●		●	●	●		●	●	●
Theravada-skolen, c/o Nils Wandel, Spangbergvn. 24b, Oslo 8.	(02) 23 67 52	Theravada									●	●	
PARAGUAY													
Reiyukai Office in Paraguay, c/o Jose F Bogado Caballero, Alvarez, Asuncion	(31) 046	Mahayana	Tsugunari Kubo	●	●		●	●	●				
PERU													
Reiyukai del Peru, Ave Javier Prado Oeste 595, Magdalena del Mar, Lima	(61) 7253	Mahayana	Tsugunari Kubo	●	●		●	●	●				

NAME & ADDRESS	TELEPHONE	TRADITION/ AFFILIATION	SPIRITUAL HEAD	Resident Teacher	City Centre	Country Centre	Regular Teachings	Meditation Facilities	Organized Retreats	Accommodation	Library	Bookshop	Newsletter
PHILIPPINES													
Karma Kagyud Dharma Centre, 5 Elgin St, South Fairview Park Subdivision, Quezon City. *Psychology & other w/shops.*		Tibetan: Vajrayana	HH Gyalwa Karmapa	●				●			●	●	
Karmapa Tantric Centre, 372 Muelle de Binondo, Room 404-406, Binondo, Manila 2805	48 88 08 46 16 61	Tibetan	Liadhianan (Lim Bu Tin)	●	●		●	●					
The Reiyukai Phillipines Office – Inner Journey, 2nd Flr Jetman Bldg, 1943 Taft Avenue Malate, Manila 2801.	(02) 521 8945. 572114		Tsugunari Kubo	●	●		●	●	●				
POLAND													
Karma Dargye Ling – Warsaw Centre, Al Zjednoczenia 11 m 43, 01-829 Warszawa.		Tibetan: Kagyu	Ole Nydahl		●	●	●	●			●		
Karma Tashi Chang Chub Ling, PO Box 1, 80-958 Gdansk 50.		Tibetan:Kagyu			●	●		●		●	●		
Karma Tenzin Ling, c/o Waldemar Zych, Poste Restante 11, 26-609 Radom. *Dance; tai chi. Psychology*		Tibetan: Kagyu	HH Gyalwa Karmapa	●	●		●	●	●	●	●	●	●
Myong-Do-Sa, Ul. Lublanska k/m 15, 31-410 Krakow		Korean Zen Chogye order	Seung-Sahn-Soen-Sa-Nim		●		●	●	●	●	●	●	
Shim Chong Sah – Gdansk Zen Centre, Grunwaldzka 121/26, 80244 Gdansk. *Psychology & other w/shops, tapes, cassettes*	41 63 99	Korean Zen (Kwan Um Zen school)	Seung-Sahn-Soen-Sa-Nim		●			●	●		●	●	●

NAME & ADDRESS	TELEPHONE	TRADITION/ AFFILIATION	SPIRITUAL HEAD	Resident Teacher	City Centre	Country Centre	Regular Teachings	Meditation Facilities	Organized Retreats	Accommodation	Library	Bookshop	Newsletter
Warsaw Zen Center, Ul. Malowiejska 24, 04-962 Warszawa – Falencia. *Psychology & other w/shops.*		Korean Zen Chogye order	Seung-Sahn-Soen Sa-Nim.			●	●	●	●	●	●	●	
Zwigzeg Buddystow Zen 'Sangha' w Polsce, Ul Noakowskiego 12m. 10, 00-666 Warszawa. *Zen w/shops*	25 61 43	Zen	Philip Kaplean		●			●	●	●	●	●	●
SINGAPORE													
Cheng Beng Buddhist Society, 20 & 24 Lorong 27a, Geylang, 1438 Singapore. *Dance: tai chi.*	748 5132 & 748 8140	Pure Land	Seck Hong Choon & Lee Kwee Hock		●		●	●	●	●	●		
SOUTH AFRICA													
The Buddhist Retreat Centre, PO Box 131, 4630 Ixopo, Natal.	Ixopo 2203	Theravada	Molly & Louis van Loon			●	●	●	●	●	●	●	●
Karma Kagyu Samye Dzong, 44 Kruger Street, Port Elisabeth, Cape 6065.	(041) 32 3112	Tibetan: Kagyu	Chuje Akong Rinpoche		●			●			●		
Karma Kagyu Samye Dzong, 4 Haven Road 3630 Westville, Durban.	(031) 85 6609	Tibetan: Kagyu	Chuje Akong Rinpoche & Kagyu Samye Ling		●			●			●		
Karma Rigdol Center, PO Box 11666, 2940 Newcastle	82500	Tibetan: Kagyu	Rob Nand					●					
Nieu Bethesda Karma Kagyu Samye Ling, PO Box 15. Nieu Bethesda, Cape 6286. *Psychology & other w/shops; pottery.*	(04923) 631	Tibetan: Kagyu				●	●	●	●	●	●		

NAME & ADDRESS	TELEPHONE	TRADITION/AFFILIATION	SPIRITUAL HEAD	Resident Teacher	City Centre	Country Centre	Regular Teachings	Meditation Facilities	Organized Retreats	Accommodation	Library	Bookshop	Newsletter
SPAIN													
C.E.T. Nagaryuna, Rosellon, 298 pral 2ª, Barcelona 37 *Psychology & other w/shops dance; tai chi; yoga.*	(3) 257 07 88	Mahayana (FPMT)	Lama Yeshe & Zopa Rinpoche	•	•		•	•			•	•	•
C.E.T. Nagaryuna, Avenida de Aster 16, Madrid 16. *Psychology & other w/shops; dance; tai chi; yoga.*	(01) 413 87 73	Mahayana (FPMT)	Lama Yeshe & Zopa Rinpoche		•		•	•			•	•	•
Despierta, c/o Princesa 3 Dpd Aptd 1736, Buzon 413, Madrid 8	242 35 74		Tsugunari Kubo	•			•	•	•				
Instituto Dharma, Motario Quintana 27, Ciudadela. (Menorca).		Tibetan: Gelug	Geshe Kelsang Gyatso				•	•					
O Sel Ling Retreat Centre, Bubión (Granada). *Centre exclusively for retreats.*	(958) 76 30 79	Mahayana (FPMT)	Lama Yeshe & Zopa Rinpoche	•		•			•	•	•	•	
Publicaciones Dharma del C.E.T. Nagaryuna, Apartado 218, Novelda, Alicante. *Buddhist publisher*		Mahayana (FPMT)	Lama Yeshe & Zopa Rinpoche										
Zen Center of Madrid, 6-2 Calle Pizarro, 13 Madrid. *Massage; Kimono-Zafu making; text translations*	231 72 98	Zen Soto	Taisen Deshimaru	•	•		•	•					•
SRI LANKA													
Aloka Viharaya, Matale, Matale District. *Psychology & other w/shops; leaf manuscripts library; script writing center.*	066-2533	Theravada	Ethipola Medankara Thero				•	•		•	•		

NAME & ADDRESS	TELEPHONE	TRADITION/ AFFILIATION	SPIRITUAL HEAD	Resident Teacher	City Centre	Country Centre	Regular Teachings	Meditation Facilities	Organized Retreats	Accommodation	Library	Bookshop	Newsletter
Buddhist Information Centre, 50 Ananda Coomaraswamy Mawatha, Colombo. *Psychology & other w/shops; Zen courses.*	23079	Theravada	Pannasiha Maha Nayaka Vipassana Thero	●	●	●	●	●	●	●	●	●	●
Island Hermitage, Polgasduwa, Galle District.		Theravada								●	●		
Mercantile Employees' Buddhist Association, 69 Kuruppu Road, 8 Colombo.		Theravada	Madihe Pannaseeha Mahanayake					●		●	●		
Nilambe Meditation Centre, Nilambe, (near Galaha)		Theravada						●		●			
Parappuduwa Nuns' Island and Meditation Centre, Dodandugoda, Dodanuwa, Galle District. *Monastery for Western Buddhist nuns. Buddhist people of female sex admitted*		Theravada	Sister Khema	●	●		●	●		●	●	●	
Purvaramaya, 47 Dias Place, 12 Colombo. *Occasional dharma teachings.*		Theravada	P Gnanarama	●							●		
Rockhill Hermitage at Wegirikanda, Hondiyadeniya, (via) Gampola.	(08) 52593	Theravada	Balangoda Ananda Maitreya Maha Nayaka Thera	●			●	●		●	●		
Walukaramaya Maha Viharaya, Pothupitiya, Wadduwa.		Theravada	Molligoda Sumanananda Thero	●			●	●		●	●		
SWEDEN													
Buddhist Centrum, c/o Detlef Schultze, Falsterbogatan 23, 21436 Malmo	(040) 97 52 29	Mahayana			●		●	●					

NAME & ADDRESS	TELEPHONE	TRADITION/ AFFILIATION	SPIRITUAL HEAD	Resident Teacher	City Centre	Country Centre	Regular Teachings	Meditation Facilities	Organized Retreats	Accommodation	Library	Bookshop	Newsletter
Buddhismens Vänner and Tibetan Friendship Group, Ringvägen 101, B, 1st Flr, 11660 Stockholm	(08) 43 53 61	All traditions	Amita Nisatta		●		●				●	●	●
Förbundet Buddhistisk Gemenskap, Box 97, Stockholm 10121	(08) 760 53 63 & 758 84 65	All traditions		●			●		●			●	
Friends of the Western Buddhist Order, Stockholm Hillbergsvägen 5, 126 54 Hägersten. *Yoga*	(08) 97 59 92	(FWBO)	Maha Sthvira Sangharakshita								●	●	●
Karma Dechen Ösel Ling, Oppeby 2546, Fellingsbro 71041		Tibetan: Karma Kagyu	HH Gyalwa Karmapa	●		●		●	●	●			
Karma Shedrup Dargye Ling, Hökarvägen 2, Hägersten 12658. *Psychology & other w/shops; Tibetan language*	(08) 88 69 50	Tibetan: Karma Kagyu	HH Gyalwa Karmapa	●	●		●	●	●				
SWITZERLAND													
Dechen Ling, Wettsteinstr 7 (PO Box 25) CH-8332 Russikon. *Psychology & other w/shops; frequent seminars*	(01) 954 02 79	All traditions	Chogyam Trungpa Rinpoche	●	●		●				●	●	●
Group D'Etudes du Dharma de Lausanne, Rue du Liseron 3, Lausanne, Vaud 1006	(021) 26 18 24	Tibetan: Kagyu/Vajradhatu						●					
Karma Tscho Phel Ling, Gerechtigkeitsgasse 9, 3011 Bern	(031) 42 61 67	Tibetan: Karma Kagyu	HH Gyalwa Karmapa		●			●			●	●	
Mahamudra Meditation Group, c/o Markus Brüderlin, Rückgasse 5, 8008 Zürich	(01) 47 65 66	Tibetan: Karma Kagyu	Namgyal Rinpoche					●	●				

NAME & ADDRESS	TELEPHONE	TRADITION/ AFFILIATION	SPIRITUAL HEAD	Resident Teacher	City Centre	Country Centre	Regular Teachings	Meditation Facilities	Organized Retreats	Accommodation	Library	Bookshop	Newsletter
Rigmed Jangchup Choeling, c/o Johannes Trischknecht, Geerenstr 1, Fehraltorf Zurich 8320. *Psychology & other w/shops* Zen Dojo – Geneva, 16 av Calas, 1206 Geneva	(01) 954 20 44	Tibetan: Gelug/ Nyingma Zen: Soto	HH The Dalai Lama	•			•	•		•	•	•	
TAIWAN													
Institute of Buddhist Studies, Hwakang Ta-en Kuan, 10th Flr. Yangmingshan, Taipei		Chinese: Chan	Dr Shen-Yen		•		•	•	•		•		
The Reiyukai, The Lay Buddhists Assocn of the Republic of China. Room 1/11FL. N0281. Sec 3. Roosevelt Rd, Taipei	(02) 394 7291/2/3		Tsugunari Kubo	•	•		•	•	•		•	•	
THAILAND													
Reiyukai Thailand Assocn, Thai Reiyukai Office, 23 Soi, 43 Sukhumut Rd, Bangkok 10110	(02) 391 0936	Non sectarian	Tsugunari Kubo				•		•				
Santi Asoke Buddhist Center, 67/1 Soi Prasartsin, Sukhaphibaani Rd. Bangapi, Klongguum, Bangkok 10240. *Printing*	377 5230		Bo-Thi-Rak-Bhikku	•	•	•	•	•	•	•		•	•
Wat Bali Lai Wun (Kow Charlart), Ampher Siracha, Chonburi 20210		Theravada	Ajahn Chai Suiy-ewo Bhikkhu	•	•	•	•	•		•	•		

NAME & ADDRESS	TELEPHONE	TRADITION/ AFFILIATION	SPIRITUAL HEAD	Resident Teacher	City Centre	Country Centre	Regular Teachings	Meditation Facilities	Organized Retreats	Accommodation	Library	Bookshop	Newsletter
UNITED KINGDOM *England*													
Anglian Buddhist Circle, c/o The Secretary, The Cottage, Moats Tye, Combs, Stowmarket, Suffolk IP14 2EX	(0449) 615819	Zen	Dr Irmgard Schloegl	●		●	●	●				●	
Baker Street Buddhist Centre, 24 Baker St, London W1	(01) 727 9382	All traditions (FWBO)	Maha Sthavira Sangharakshita		●		●	●	●			●	●
Bath Buddhist Group, 12 Station Rd, Bath, Avon	(0225) 337918	All traditions				●	●						
Berkshire Buddhist Society, 92 Brighton Rd, Earley, Reading, Berkshire. *Assocd with Chithurst Monastery*	(0734) 662817	Theravada/ Zen											
Birmingham Buddhist Vihara & Soto Zen Meditation Group, 47 Carlyle Rd, Edgbaston, Birmingham B16 9BH	(021) 454 6591	Theravada	Dr Rewata Dharma	●	●		●	●	●	●	●	●	●
Birmingham Karma Ling, 41 Carlyle Rd, Edgbaston, Birmingham B16 9BH	(021) 454 2782	Tibetan: Kagyu	Lama Thubten/HH Gyalwa Karmapa	●	●		●	●	●				●
Bournemouth & District Buddhist group, 36 Wheaton Rd, Pokesdown, Bournemouth, Dorset BH7 6LJ. *Tai chi*	(0202) 510872 & (0202) 422342	Mahayana, Zen Theravada					●						
Bradford Buddhist Group, c/o 15 Selbourne Terrace, Shipley, West Yorkshire, BD18 3BZ	(0274) 59 0279	All traditions					●						
Brighton Buddhist Centre, 15 Park Crescent Place, Brighton, East Sussex, BN2 3HF. *Yoga; karate; art & cultural activities*	(0273) 698420	(FWBO)	Maha Sthavira Sangharakshita	●	●		●	●	●	●	●	●	●
British Buddhist Assocn, 57 Farringdon Rd, London EC1M 3JB. *Pali language; provides speakers*	(01) 242 5538 (office hours)	All traditions			●		●				●	●	

NAME & ADDRESS	TELEPHONE	TRADITION/ AFFILIATION	SPIRITUAL HEAD	Resident Teacher	City Centre	Country Centre	Regular Teachings	Meditation Facilities	Organized Retreats	Accommodation	Library	Bookshop	Newsletter
British Mahabodhi Society/London Buddhist Vihara, 5 Heathfield Gdns, Chiswick, London W4 4JU	(01) 995 9493	Theravada	Dr H Saddhatis-sa	●	●		●	●	●		●	●	●
British Shingon Buddhist Assocn, 58 Mansfield Rd London NW8. *Psychology & other w/shops*	(01) 486 7313	Chinese		●	●		●		●		●	●	●
Buddhapadipa Temple, 14 Calonne Rd, Wimbledon Parkside, London SW19 55H	(01) 946 1357	Theravada		●	●			●	●	●	●	●	●
Buddha Vihara, 84 Dacre Rd, Plaistow, London, E13 0PR. *Free legal advice*	(01) 472 6333	Theravada	Dr Ambedkar	●			●	●				●	
The Buddhist Centre, Oaken Holt, Farmoor, Oxford, OX2 9NL	(08676) 2231	Theravada	Myat Saw	●	●	●	●	●	●	●	●	●	●
The Buddhist Society, 58 Eccleston Sq, SW1V 1PH *Qrtly journal; cassettes*	(01) 834 5858	All traditions	To be appointed		●		●	●	●		●	●	●
Cambridge Buddhist Society, 42 Kingston St, Cambridge	(0223) 51046						●		●		●	●	
Cheltenham Buddhist Society, c/o Mrs Jean Thompson, 35 Hurran Gardens, Churchdown, Gloucester	(0452) 856337								●				
Chesterfield Soto Buddhist Group, 75 Hucknall Ave, Ashgate, Chesterfield, Derbyshire	(0246) 70686	Soto Zen											
Chichester Buddhist Society, 25 Oving Village, Nr Chichester, West Sussex. *Tai chi*	(0243) 784648	Soto Zen/ Tibetan				●	●	●	●		●		
Ching Kang Lung Szu, London Rd, East Dereham, Norfolk NR19 1AJ. *Chinese yoga; kempo; translation & research*	(0862) 3962	Chinese: Chen Yen	Achali Ching Kang Szu	●		●	●	●	●	●	●	●	●

NAME & ADDRESS	TELEPHONE	TRADITION/AFFILIATION	SPIRITUAL HEAD	Resident Teacher	City Centre	Country Centre	Regular Teachings	Meditation Facilities	Organized Retreats	Accommodation	Library	Bookshop	Newsletter
Chithurst Forest Monastery, Chithurst House, Nr Petersfield, Hampshire GU31 5EU	(073 081) 4986	Theravada	Sumedho Bhikku	•		•	•	•	•	•	•		•
Croydon Buddhist Centre, 96-98 High St, Croydon, Surrey CRO 1ND. *Psychology & other w/shops; yoga; cultural activities; residential communities*	(01) 688 8624	(FWBO)	Maha Sthavira Sangharakshita	•	•		•	•	•				
Dharma Dipa, c/o 'Owls' Roost', 38 Orton Ave, Sutton Coldfield, West Midlands B Y6 8JJ	(021) 351 1966	Tibetan	Chögyam Trungpa Rinpoche				•	•			•		
Dharma House Trust, Gilly Lane, Whitecross, Penzance, Cornwall TR20 8BZ	(0736) 740759	Soto Zen				•	•	•	•	•	•		
(Osel Choling) Dharma Study Group, 17 Marius Rd, London SW17	(01) 673 6115	Tibetan: Kagyu/Nyingma	Chögyam Trungpa Rinpoche	•	•		•	•	•		•		
(Osel Choling) Dharma Study Group, 36 Archfield Rd, Lotham, Bristol, Gloucestershire BS6 5BE	(0272) 46266 &	Tibetan: Kagyu/Nyingma	Chögyam Trungpa Rinpoche	•	•		•	•	•		•		
(Osel Choling) Dharma Study Group, Vajradhatu, Elwyn Maddy, Llanigon, Hay-on-Wye, Hereford. HR3 5QE	(049 74) 336	Tibetan: Kagyu	Chögyam Trungpa Rinpoche	•		•	•	•	•	•			•
Doncaster Buddhist Group, 9 Avenue Rd, Wheatley, Doncaster, South Yorks, DN 4AH	(0302) 60308	Theravada		•		•	•	•	•	•	•		
Durham University Buddhist Society, 11 Station Rd, Leamside, Houghton-le-Spring. DH4 6SE. *Yoga; & Jin Shin Do*	(0783) 845971	All traditions		•			•	•					
Dzogchen Community, 12 Greenway Gdns, London NW3. Mailing address only. *Yantra yoga; weekly puja.*		Tibetan	Namkai Norbu Rinpoche		•		•	•	•			•	•

NAME & ADDRESS	TELEPHONE	TRADITION/ AFFILIATION	SPIRITUAL HEAD	Resident Teacher	City Centre	Country Centre	Regular Teachings	Meditation Facilities	Organized Retreats	Accommodation	Library	Bookshop	Newsletter
Eden Valley Buddhist Group, Fernlea, Ruckcroft, Nr Armathwaite, Carlisle, Cumbria CA4 9QR		Theravada						●					
Ekayano, 28 Glovers Lane, Heelands, Milton Keynes, Buckinghamshire MK13 7LW. *Psychology & other w/shops*	(0908) 319256	Western			●			●				●	
Essex Buddhist Society, c/o 134 Long Riding, Basildon, Essex	(0268) 26346	All traditions						●					
Foresight, 29 Beaufort Avenue, Hodge Hill, Birmingham B34 6AD. *Magazine*	(021) 783 0587					●		●					
Friends of the Western Buddhists Order Top Flr, 24 Baker St, London W1. *Psychology; massage; residential communities*	(01) 258 3706 & (01) 328 1578	(FWBO)	Maha Sthavira Sangharakshita	●	●		●	●	●	●		●	●
FWBO Bristol, 120 Long Ashton Rd. Long Ashton, Bristol, Avon	(0272) 39 2463	(FWBO)	Maha Sthavira Sangharakshita		●		●	●	●			●	
Friends of the Western Buddhist Order, 18 Burlington Rd. Withington, Manchester M20 92A. *Residential Communities*		(FWBO)	Maha Sthavira Sangharakshita	●	●		●	●	●	●		●	
FWBO Leeds, 51 Harehills Ave. Leeds LS2	(0532) 486036	(FWBO)	Maha Sthavira Sangharakshita	●	●		●	●	●	●		●	
Gillets Community, Smorden, nr Ashford, Kent	(0233) 77224	Theravada				●	●	●					
Hampstead Buddhist Group, c/o The Secretary, 4 Teynham Court, Woodside Ave. London N12 8AU	(01) 446 0132	Theravada Chithurst Mnsry	Sumedho Bikkhu				●	●	●		●		
Hampshire Buddhist Society, 1 The Broadway, Winchester, Hampshire	(0962) 61194	Theravada Chithurst Mnsry	Sumedho Bikkhu				●	●	●		●	●	

NAME & ADDRESS	TELEPHONE	TRADITION/ AFFILIATION	SPIRITUAL HEAD	Resident Teacher	City Centre	Country Centre	Regular Teachings	Meditation Facilities	Organized Retreats	Accommodation	Library	Bookshop	Newsletter
Harnham Vihara, 2 Harnham Hall Cottages, Harnham, nr Belsay, Northumberland NE20 0HF	(066 181) 612	Theravada Chithurst Mnsry	Sumedho Bikkhu			•		•					
Hastings Buddhist Society, Tongs Hse, Pett Level Hastings, E Sussex TN35 4EE	(042486) 3176	Zen				•		•					
Heart of England Buddhist Group, 43 Manor Rd, Harbury, Leamington Spa, Warwickshire CV33 9HY	(0926) 613507	Tibetan/ Theravada	Sogyal Rinpoche Khemadhammo Bikkhu				•						
Herefordshire Buddhist Group, Canon Frome Crt, nr Ledbury, Herefordshire	(053 183) 306	Theravada	Khemadhammo Bikkhu				•						
Household Buddhist Group, Penaluna, Clodgy Moor, Penzance, Cornwall, TR19 6UR *Works with Dharma House Trust*	(0736) 73449	Soto Zen				•							
House of Inner Tranquility, 10 Masons Lane, Bradford on Avon, Wiltshire BA15 1ON	(022 16) 6821	Theravada				•							
Hull Buddhist Group, c/o Carl Stephenson, 23 Bachelor St, Saner St, Anlaby Rd, Hull	(0482) 217997						•						
Indian Buddhist Society of the UK Nanda Hse, 9 Carlisle Rd, Edgbaston, Birmingham B16 9BM	(021) 455 7285	Theravada		•		•	•	•	•	•			
Insight Assocn, East Farm Hse, Wylye, Warminster, Wiltshire. *Psychology & other w/shops; backpacking; massage; yoga & life issues*	(0985) 6241	Vipassana	Christopher Titmuss & Christina Feldman			•	•	•	•	•	•		•
International Meditation Centre UK, (Savaji UBA Khin Memorial Trust), Splatts Hse, Heddington, nr Calne. Wiltshire SN11 0PE	(0380) 850238	Theravada				•	•						

NAME & ADDRESS	TELEPHONE	TRADITION/ AFFILIATION	SPIRITUAL HEAD	Resident Teacher	City Centre	Country Centre	Regular Teachings	Meditation Facilities	Organized Retreats	Accommodation	Library	Bookshop	Newsletter
Jodo Shu Foundation of Gt Britain, 48 Laburnum Cres, Kettering, Northants NN16 9PJ. Children's programme	(0536) 517782	Japanese Pure Land				•							
Kampo Gangra Kagyu Ling, 1a Reynard Rd, Chorlton, Manchester M21 2DB.	(061) 881 5221	Tibetan: Karma Kagyu	Karma Thinley	•			•	•	•		•	•	•
Karma Kagyu Chokhor Ling, c/o Mike Barnett, Flat 1, 60 Savernake Rd, London NW3 2JP	(01) 485 9897	Tibetan:	Chime Rinpoche		•								
Kham Tibetan House, Chos Khorling, 2 Rectory Lane, Ashdon, nr Saffron Walden Essex CB10 2HM	(0799) 84415	Tibetan	Lama Chime Rinpoche			•		•		•			
Kongoryuji, 29 London Rd, East Dereham, Norfolk NR19 1AS. *Chinese Yoga: Buddhist kempo: cheirology*		Chinese Shingon	Fa Tao Meng (Taiwan)	•	•		•	•	•		•	•	•
Kongoryuji, (London), 58 Mansfield Rd, London NW3 *kempo: Chinese Yoga*		Chinese Shingon	Shifu T Dukes & Acarya Ryushu Otomo Shifu Nagaboshi Tomio	•	•		•	•			•	•	•
Kongoryuji, (Norwich) 2 Stanmore Rd, Thorpe St Andrew, Norwich. *Chinese yoga: cheirology: kempo*		Chinese Shingon					•	•					
Lancaster University Buddhist Society, c/o Imelda C Alldiss, 20 Willow Grove, Pormby, Merseyside L37 3NX		All traditions			•								
Leeds Buddhist Group, c/o David Evans, 43a Templegate Rd, Leeds LS15 0HF		All traditions				•							
Leicester Buddhist Society, 6 Half Moon Crescent, Oadby, Leicester. *Abidharma*	(0533) 712339				•								
Liverpool Buddhist Group, 39 Gorsedale Rd, Liverpool L18 5Ey. *Regular Meetings*	(051) 734 1371	Theravada			•		•	•			•	•	•

NAME & ADDRESS	TELEPHONE	TRADITION/ AFFILIATION	SPIRITUAL HEAD	Resident Teacher	City Centre	Country Centre	Regular Teachings	Meditation Facilities	Organized Retreats	Accom-modation	Library	Bookshop	Newsletter
London Buddhist Centre, 51 Roman Rd, London E2 0HU. *Psychology & other w/shops; dance, tai chi; communities; co-operatives; aid for India; registered charity*	(01) 981 1225	(FWBO)	Maha Sthavira Sangharakshita	●	●		●	●	●		●	●	●
London Buddhist Vihara, 5 Heathfield Gdns London W4 4JU	(01) 995 9493	Theravada	Dr H Saddhatissa	●	●		●	●			●	●	●
London Dhamma Group, 32 King Henry's Rd, London NW3. *Dhamma studies*	(01) 586 5416	Theravada					●						
London Zen Society, 10 Belmont St, London NW1 8HH. *Visiting teachers*	(01) 485 9576	Zen Rinzai			●		●						
Madhyamaka Centre, 15 Clifford St, York, Yorkshire	(0904) 35095 & 706038	Mahayana	Geshe Kelsang Gyatso		●		●		●			●	
Magga Bhavaka, 30 Devonshire Place, Jesmond, Newcastle upon Tyne, NE2 2ND	(0632) 811328	Theravada			●		●						
Manchester Buddhist Centre, 18 Burlington Rd, Withington, Manchester	(061) 445 3806	Harnham Vihara (FWBO)	Maha Sthavira Sangharakshita	●	●		●	●	●		●	●	
Manchester University Buddhist Society, University Union, Oxford Rd, Manchester M13 9PL. *Regular mtgs*	(061) 273 3333						●						
Manjushri Institute, Conishead Priory, Ulverston, Cumbria LA12 9QQ. *Psychology & other w/shops; group trng facility; tourism facility; dance; tai chi*	(0229) 54029	Mahayana (FPMT)	Lama Yeshe & Zopa Rinpoche	●		●	●	●	●	●	●	●	
Manjushri London Centre, 10 Finsbury Park Rd, London N4. *Psychology & other w/shops*	(01) 359 1394	Mahayana (FPMT)	Lama Yeshe & Zopa Rinpoche	●	●		●	●	●		●	●	
Marpa Institute, East Barton, nr Bury St Edmunds, Suffolk				●									

NAME & ADDRESS	TELEPHONE	TRADITION/ AFFILIATION	SPIRITUAL HEAD	Resident Teacher	City Centre	Country Centre	Regular Teachings	Meditation Facilities	Organized Retreats	Accommodation	Library	Bookshop	Newsletter
Mid Kent and Medway Buddhist Group, 5 Allington Way, Maidstone, Kent ME16 0HJ. *Visiting teachers*	(0622) 671512	Theravada				●	●				●		
Mid Sussex Buddhist Group, c/o Roy Brabant Smith, 108a Junction Rd, Burgess Hill, Sussex RH15 0NU *Visiting teachers*	(04446) 46300 (04446) 5309	Theravada				●							
Milton Keynes Buddhist Group, 28 Glovers Lane, Heelands, Milton Keynes, Bucks	(0908) 319256	All traditions					●						
Naradipa Vihara – Isle of Wight Buddhist Fellowship, Springvale, Furrlongs, Newport Isle of Wight PO30 2AA	(0983) 529839	Theravada	Khemadhammo Bhikkhu	●	●		●	●		●	●	●	●
Nichiren Shonen of UK, 1 The Green, Richmond, Surrey. *Regular Meetings at members' homes; member of 'Sokagakkai International'*	(01) 948 0381/2	Mahayana Japanese lay peoples soc	Nichiren Daishonen										
North Staffordshire Zazen Group, 21 Longton Rd, Trentham, Stoke on Trent, Staffordshire ST4 8ND *Regular mtgs*	(0782) 657851	Soto Zen									●		
Norwich Meditation Centre, Friends of the Western Buddhist Order, 41a All Saints Green, Norwich, Norfolk. *Yoga; massage; communications*	(0603) 27034	(FWBO)	Maha Sthavira Sangharakshita	●	●		●	●	●		●	●	●
Nottingham & District Buddhist Society, 26 Millicent Rd, West Bridgford, Nottingham. *Regular mtgs*		Soto Zen			●								
Oxford Buddhist Centre, 48 James St, Oxford	(0865) 245283	All traditions	Chogyam Trungpa Rinpoche	●	●		●	●	●				

NAME & ADDRESS	TELEPHONE	TRADITION/ AFFILIATION	SPIRITUAL HEAD	Resident Teacher	City Centre	Country Centre	Regular Teachings	Meditation Facilities	Organized Retreats	Accom- modation	Library	Bookshop	Newsletter
Padma Choling, 68 Blenheim Grove, Peckham, London SE15 4QL. *Mainly language w/shops*	(01) 732 0183	Indian/ Tibetan			•		•				•		
Padmaloka Men's Retreat Centre, Lessingham Hse, Surlingham, nr Norwich, Norfolk NR14 7AL. *Psychology; yoga massage*	(050 88) 8112	FWBO	Maha Sthavira Sangharakshita	•		•		•	•	•	•		
Petersfield Buddhist Group, 8 St Peter's Rd, Petersfield, Hampshire GU32 3HX. *Regular mtgs*	(0730) 3040	Soto Zen				•							
Reiyukai (Liverpool), 1 Huntly Rd, Liverpool, Lancashire L6 3AJ	(051) 2649568	Reiyukai	Tsugunari Kubo				•						
Reiyukai (Norwich), 196 Unthank Rd, Norwich, Norfolk NR2 2AH	(0603) 501151	Reiyukai	Tsugunari Kubo	•	•		•	•	•	•	•		•
Rigpa, 44 St Paul's Crescent, London NW1 9TN. *Psychology & other w/shops dance; tai chi; yoga; children's dharma class; cassette correspondence*	(01) 485 4342	All traditions esp Nyingma	Lama Sogyal Rinpoche	•	•		•	•	•		•	•	•
Sakya Thinley Rinchen Ling, 27 Lilymead Ave, Knowle, Bristol BS4 2BY. *Thinley Soc for Children*	(0272) 712961	Tibetan: Sakya	Karma Thinley Rinpoche	•	•		•	•	•	•		•	•
Samatha Assocn/Samatha Trust, 21 High Lane, Charlton, Manchester M21 1DJ, Lancashire	(061) 8607110	Theravada		•	•		•	•	•				
Samye Dzong, 20 Northumberland Ave, Gosforth, Newcastle upon Tyne	(0632) 852240	Tibetan: Kagyu	Akong Rinpoche	•	•		•	•					

NAME & ADDRESS	TELEPHONE	TRADITION/ AFFILIATION	SPIRITUAL HEAD	Resident Teacher	City Centre	Country Centre	Regular Teachings	Meditation Facilities	Organized Retreats	Accommodation	Library	Bookshop	Newsletter
Scientific Buddhist Assocn, 30 Hollingbourne Gdns, Ealing, London W13 8EN. *Support for persecuted Buddhists; correspondence, meditation*	(01) 998 8368	All traditions						•					•
Shin Buddhist Assocn, Wessex Hills, 92b Chapmanslade, Westbury, BA13 4AN. *Journal–Western Buddhist; funerals; weddings*	(0373) 88282	Mahayana	HE Koshin Ohtani & Nishi Hongwan Ji									•	•
South Devon Buddhist Group, c/o Stancombe Linhays, Ashprington, Totnes, Devon TQ9 7DY	(080) 423 651	Theravada (Chithurst)	Sumedho Bikkhu			•		•	•	•			•
Sunderland Polytechnic Buddhist Meditation Soc, c/o Students Union, Chester Rd, Sunderland. *Tel c/o Peter Harvey after 6pm*	(0385) 43913												
Thames Buddhist Vihara & Meditation Centre, Memorial Hall, Dulverton Rd, Selsdon, Surrey	(01) 657 7120	Theravada		•		•	•	•					
Throssel Hole Monastery, Carrshield, Hexham, Northumberland NE47 8AL	(049 85) 204	Soto Zen	Rev Roshi Jiyu Kennett	•		•	•	•	•	•		•	•
Tyneside Zen Buddhist Group, 246 Wharton Trrce, Heaton, Newcastle upon Tyne. *Regular mtgs*	(0632) 761096	Soto Zen											
University of Kent Buddhist Society, c/o Zamantha Walker, 19 Manor Rd, Tankerton Whitstable, Kent. *Regular mtgs.*													

NAME & ADDRESS	TELEPHONE	TRADITION/ AFFILIATION	SPIRITUAL HEAD	Resident Teacher	City Centre	Country Centre	Regular Teachings	Meditation Facilities	Organized Retreats	Accom- modation	Library	Bookshop	Newsletter
Vipassana Meditation Centre, Chapter Hse, Gorefield Rd, Leverington, Wisbech, Cambridgeshire PE135AS. *Dance, tai chi & yoga*	(0045) 583838	Theravada		•		•	•	•	•	•		•	•
Weymouth Buddhist Group, 8 Connaught Rd, Weymouth, Dorset. *Tai chi; regular mtgs*	(0305) 78658	Zen & Theravada											
Wolverhampton Buddhist Vihara, 146 Lea Rd, Wolverhampton WV3 0LQ. *Sunday School*	(0902) 341296	Theravada		•	•		•	•	•	•	•	•	
Worcester Buddhist Centre – Karma Yong dus Chopel Ling, 110 Lansdowne Rd, Worcester, Worcestershire WR3 8JL. *Spiritual healing*	(0905) 20104	Tibetan			•		•	•					
UNITED KINGDOM Northern Ireland													
Asanga Institute, 75 Knutsford Dr, Cliftonville Rd, Belfast BT14 6NA	(0232) 75 4623	Mahayana (FPMT)	Lama Yeshe & Zopa Rinpoche		•			•			•	•	
UNITED KINGDOM Scotland													
Edinburgh Buddhist Group, 7 Bruntsfield Grdns, Edinburgh, Lothian EH10 4DX. *Regular Mtgs*	(031) 229 6011	Theravada			•								

NAME & ADDRESS	TELEPHONE	TRADITION/ AFFILIATION	SPIRITUAL HEAD	Resident Teacher	City Centre	Country Centre	Regular Teachings	Meditation Facilities	Organized Retreats	Accommodation	Library	Bookshop	Newsletter
Glasgow Buddhist Centre, 329 Sauchiehall St, Glasgow G2. *Psychology & other w/shops; residential communities*	(041) 333 0524	(FWBO)	Maha Sthavira Sangharakshita	●	●		●	●	●			●	
Kagyu Samye Ling, Eskdalemuir, nr Langholm, Dumfriesshire DG13 9QL. *Psychology & other w/shops; dance & tai chi*	(05416) 232	Tibetan; Kagyu	HH Gyalwa Karmapa	●		●	●	●	●		●	●	●
Osel Choling Dharma Study Group, 10 Glencairn Crescent, Edinburgh EH12 5BS	(031) 225 1895	Tibetan: Kagyu	Chogyam Trungpa Rinpoche	●	●			●			●		
St Andrews Buddhist group, 5 Park St, St Andrews, Fife, Scotland	(0334) 75944	Theravada											
UNITED KINGDOM *Wales*													
Aberystwyth Buddhist Group, Gelli Padarn, Pen-y-Craig Hill, Llanbadarn, Aberystwyth	(0970) 615285												
Cardiff Buddhist Community, 97a Albany Rd, Roath, Cardiff CF2 3LP													
Kampo Gangra Dechen Ling, 11 Montpelier Trce, Mount Pleasant, Swansea SA1 6JW	(0792) 464217	Tibetan: Kagyu	Karma Thinley Rinpoche	●	●		●	●	●			●	●
Lam Rim Buddhist Group, Milarepa Hse, 51 Ferry Rd, Grangetown, Cardiff CF1 7DW. *Regular mtgs*		Tibetan	Geshe Damcho Yonten										
Lam Rim Buddhist Centre, Pentwyn Manor, Penrhos, nr Raglan, Gwent NP5 2CE. *Dance & tai chi*	(0660) 085383	Tibetan	Geshe Damcho Yonten	●			●	●	●			●	

NAME & ADDRESS	TELEPHONE	TRADITION/ AFFILIATION	SPIRITUAL HEAD	Resident Teacher	City Centre	Country Centre	Regular Teachings	Meditation Facilities	Organized Retreats	Accommodation	Library	Bookshop	Newsletter
Sang Ngak Cho Dzang, 20 Connaught Rd, Roath, Cardiff CF2 3PT, S Glamorgan	(0222) 495539	Tibetan: Nyingma	Dudjom Rinpoche & Yeshe Dorje Rinpoche	●	●		●	●			●		
Vajraloka, The Buddhist Meditation Centre of N Wales, Tyn-y-Ddol, Corwen, Clwyd LL21 0EN. *Full time intensive meditation retreat*	(0490 81) 406	(FWBO)	Maha Sthavira Sangharakshita			●		●	●	●			
USA Alaska													
Khawachen Dharma Center, PO Box 10-1283, Anchorage, AK 99510 *Visiting teachers*	(907) 279 0376	Rimay	Nodup Paljor (advisor)		●			●			●		●
USA California													
Buddhist Circle for Peace, 2490 Channing Way, Rm 503, Berkeley, CA 94709. *Ceremonies buttons; tee shirts*	(415) 843 2127	Ekayana		●	●		●	●		●	●	●	●
Buddhist Vihara of Los Angeles, 1147 North Beachwood Dr, CA 90038. *Psychology & other w/shops*	(213) 464 9698	Theravada	Pandit Ahangama Dhammarana		●		●	●					●
Cimarron Zen Center of Rinzai-Ji, 2505 Cimarron St, Los Angeles CA 90018	(213) 732 2263	Zen	Joshu Sasaki Roshi				●	●					
City of 10,000 Buddhas, PO Box 217, Talmage, CA 95481	(707) 462 0939	Mahayana	Tripitaka Master Hsuan Hua	●			●	●	●	●	●	●	●

NAME & ADDRESS	TELEPHONE	TRADITION/ AFFILIATION	SPIRITUAL HEAD	Resident Teacher	City Centre	Country Centre	Regular Teachings	Meditation Facilities	Organized Retreats	Accommodation	Library	Bookshop	Newsletter
Davis Dharma Study Group, 1108 Cypress Lane, Davis, CA 95616	(916) 758 3576	Tibetan: Kagyu	Chogyam Trungpa Rinpoche				●	●			●		
Dharmadhatu, 2288 Fulton St, Berkeley, CA 94704	(415) 841 3242	Tibetan: Kagyu	Chogyam Trungpa Rinpoche	●			●	●			●	●	
Dharma Study Group, 434 Maple Lane, Garberville, CA 95440	(707) 923 3891	Kagyu & Zen	Chogyam Trungpa Rinpoche				●	●			●		
Dharma Study Group of San Diego, c/o Nancy Porter Steele. 1087 Pine Dr, El Cajon, CA 92020	(619) 442 4183	Vajrayana Kagyu	Chogyam Trungpa Rinpoche					●					
Empty Gate Zen Center, 1800 Arch St, Berkeley, CA 94709		Korean	Master Seung Sahn	●	●		●		●	●	●	●	●
Gelugpa Society of Yamantaka 1439 'E' St, Napa, CA 94559		Slavic Mongolian (Tibet)	Dilowa Karanov	●		●	●						●
Gold Wheel Monastery, 1728 Sixth St, Los Angeles CA 90017	(213) 483 7497	Mahayana	Tripitaka Master Hsuan Hua	●			●	●	●	●		●	●
Gold Mountain Monastery, 1731-15th St, San Francisco, CA 94103	(415) 861 9672 & (415) 626 4204	Mahayana	Tripiaka Master Hsuan Hua						●	●		●	●
Hartford Street Zen Center, 57 Hartford, San Francisco, CA 94114	(415) 863 2507	Zen	Issan Dorsey	●					●				●
'Inner Trip Friends', The Reiyukai, American Reiyukai Office, 2741 Sunset Blvd, Los Angeles, CA 90026	(213) 413 1771		Tsugunari Kubo										
International Buddhist Meditation Center, 928 South, New Hampshire Ave. CA 90006 Psychology & other w/shops	(213) 384 0850	Zen Lam Te	Karuna Dharma	●	●	●	●	●	●	●	●	●	●
International Institute for the Translation of Buddhist Texts, 3636 Washington St, San Francisco CA 94118	(415) 921 9570	Mahayana	Tripitaka Mstr Hsuan Hua	●			●					●	

NAME & ADDRESS	TELEPHONE	TRADITION/ AFFILIATION	SPIRITUAL HEAD	Resident Teacher	City Centre	Country Centre	Regular Teachings	Meditation Facilities	Organized Retreats	Accommodation	Library	Bookshop	Newsletter
Joshu Zen Temple, 2303 Harriman Lane, Redondo Beach, CA 90278		Zen		●	●		○	●	●	●	●	●	●
Kagyu Donga Chuling, 4949 Elmwood Ave, Los Angeles, CA 90004	(213) 464 2489	Tibetan	Kalu Rinpoche	●	●		●	●	●				
Kagyu Shangpa Chöling, 2251 S Refugio Rd, Gobeta, CA 93117	(805) 968 2110	Kagyu	Kalu Rinpoche	●	●	●		●	●				
Karma Thegsum Chöling, 5900 Claremont Ave, Oakland, CA 94618	(415) 653 2568	Kagyu	HH Gyalwa Karmapa					●	●				
Kannon-Do, 292 College Ave, Mt View, CA 94041	(415) 948 5020	Soto Zen	Suzuki Roshi (deceased)	●			●	●	●		●		●
Middlebar Buddhist Monastary, 2503 Del Rio Dr, CA 95204. *Seminary*		Soto Zen				●	●	●	●	●	●		
Mr Baldy Zen Center, PO Box 429, CA 91759	(714) 985 6410	Zen		●	●	●	●	●	●	●			
Nyingma Institute, 1815 Highland Plce, Berkeley, CA 94709. *Psychology & other w/shops; Kum nye trg*	(415) 843 6812	Tibetan: Nyingma	Tarthang Tulku	●	●	●	●	●	●	●	●	●	●
Rigpa, PO Box 7326, Santa Cruz, CA 95061. *Psychology & other w/shops*	(408) 688 2208	Tibetan	Lama Sogyal Rinpoche	●			●	●	●				●
Santa Cruz Karma Thegsum Chöling PO Box 8059, Santa Cruz, CA 95061	(408) 426 6179	Tibetan	HH Gyalwa Karmapa			●	●	●	●	●	●	●	
Society of the Smiling Buddha, 454 Marine St, La Jolla, CA 92037		Zen		●	●			●	●			●	●
Shasta Abbey, Hqtrs of Order of Buddhist Contemplatives of the Soto Zen Church, PO Box 199, Mt Shasta, CA 96067. *Priest trg program; Buddhist supplies; cemetary & Columbarium*	(916) 926 4208	Soto Zen	Roshi Jiyu-kennett OBC	●	●	●	●	●	●	●	●	●	●

NAME & ADDRESS	TELEPHONE	TRADITION/ AFFILIATION	SPIRITUAL HEAD	Resident Teacher	City Centre	Country Centre	Regular Teachings	Meditation Facilities	Organized Retreats	Accommodation	Library	Bookshop	Newsletter
Taungpulu Kaba-Aye Monastery, 18335 Big Basin Way, Boulder Creek, CA 95006.	(408) 338 4050	Theravada	Ven Taungpulu Sayadaw (when here); Ven Hlaingtet Sayadaw	●		●		●	●	●	●		●
Thubten Dhargye Ling, 135 North St Andrews Pl, Los Angeles CA 90004	(213) 466 2310	Gelug	Geshe Tsultrim Gyeltsen	●	●		●	●	●		●		●
Vajrapani Institute, PO Box I, Kings Creek Rd, Boulder Creek, CA 95006	(408) 338 6654	Mahayana (FPMT)	Lama Yeshe & Zopa Rinpoche	●		●	●	●	●	●	●	●	
USA Colorado.													
Boulder Zen Center, 1139 12th St, Boulder, CO 80302		Zen		●		●		●	●	●	●		
Rocky Mountain Dharma Centre, Red Feather Lakes, CO 80545. *Psychology & other w/shops; hosts other grps; solitary rituals*	(303) 881 2530	Tibetan: Kagyu/Nyingma	Chogyam Trungpa Rinpoche	●	●	●	●	●	●	●	●	●	●
Shambhala Training, 2130 Arapahoe Ave, 2nd Flr, Boulder, CO 80302. *Psychology & other w/shops; weekend programmes*	(303) 444 7881	Shambhala	Chogyam Trungpa Rinpoche		●	●	●	●	●				
USA Connecticut													
New Haven Zen Center Inc, 193 Mansfield St, New Haven CT 06511. *Psychology & other w/shops*	(203) 787 0912	Zen	Master Seung Sahn	●	●		●	●	●	●	●	●	●

NAME & ADDRESS	TELEPHONE	TRADITION/ AFFILIATION	SPIRITUAL HEAD	Resident Teacher	City Centre	Country Centre	Regular Teachings	Meditation Facilities	Organized Retreats	Accommodation	Library	Bookshop	Newsletter
USA *Hawaii*													
Dharma Buddhist Temple of Hawaii, 1294 Kalani-Iki St, Honolulu, Hawaii 96817. *Limited library*	(808) 373 3337	Mahayana	Master Danette V Choi, PHD	●	●		●	●	●				●
Kagyu Theg Chen Ling, 2327 Liloa Rise, Honolulu, Hawaii 96822. *Psychology & other w/shops dance; tai chi*	(808) 941 8561	Tibetan	Kalu Rinpoche		●		●	●	●	●	●	●	●
Kagyu Thubten Choling, PO Box 639 Kilavea, Kavai, Hawaii 96754. *Visitors welcome*	(808) 828 1548	Tibetan	Kalu Rinpoche			●	●	●			●		
Ko Ko An Zendo of the Diamond Sangha, 2119 Kaba Way, Honolulu, Hawaii 98622. *Psychology & other w/shops*	(808) 946 0666	Zen	Robert Aitken Roshi		●		●	●	●		●		●
Mavi Zendo of the Diamond Sangha, 911 Kaupakalua Rd, Haiku, Hawaii 96708	(808) 572 8103	Zen	Robert Aitken Roshi			●	●	●			●	●	
Nechung Dorje Drayang Ling, PO Box 250, Pahala, Hawaii 96777. *Psychology & other w/shops*	(808) 928 8539	Tibetan		●		●	●	●	●	●	●	●	●
The Sudatta Society, PO Box 17006, Honolulu, Hawaii 96817	(808) 847 0025	Mahayana										●	
USA *Idaho*													
The Open Path, A Center for Eastern and Western Studies, 703 North 18th St, ID 83702. *Psychology & other w/shops; movement & publishing*	(208) 342 0208	Tibetan: Karma Kagyu	Tenzin Dorje & Namgyal Rinpoche	●	●		●	●	●		●	●	●

NAME & ADDRESS	TELEPHONE	TRADITION/ AFFILIATION	SPIRITUAL HEAD	Resident Teacher	City Centre	Country Centre	Regular Teachings	Meditation Facilities	Organized Retreats	Accommodation	Library	Bookshop	Newsletter
USA *Illinois*													
The Buddhist Temple of Chicago, 1151 W Leland Ave, Chicago, IL 60640. *Psychology; judo; kendo; scouts & study centre*	(334) 4661 & 2	Mahayana	Gyomay M Kubose	●	●		●	●	●	●	●	●	●
Chicago Meditation Center, c/o D Joshi, 5049 N Major 1, Chicago, IL 60630 *Regular class*	(312) 286 4699 (312) 545 6723	Vipassana & Zen			●				●				
Thai Buddhist Temple, New: 7059 W 75th St, Chicago, IL 60638. *Psychology & other w/shops; Monday school; cultural centre*	(312) 458 9676 (312) 496 9671	Theravada	Phra Sudhirata-naporn	●	●	●	●	●	●		●		●
USA *Maryland*													
American Zen College, 16815 Germantown Rd, Germantown MD 20874	(301) 428 0665	Zen Korean Mahayana	Master Gosung Shin PhD	●		●	●	●	●	●	●	●	●
The Cambodian Buddhist Temple, 6301 Westbrook Dr, New Carrollton, MD 20784	(301) 577 7596	Theravada	Oung Mean Canavanna	●		●	●	●		●	●	●	●
USA *Massachusetts*													
American Institute of Buddhist Studies, 61 Lincoln Ave, Amherst, MA 01002 *Psychology & other w/shops; translation projects; Tibetan Medicine*	(413) 549 6893	Non Sectarian		●			●				●	●	
Boston Buddhist Center, 470 Centre St, Boston, MA 02130 *Psychology & other w/shops; resident community*	(617) 522 0336	Western (FWBO)	Maha Sthavira Sangharakshita	●	●		●	●	●		●	●	●

NAME & ADDRESS	TELEPHONE	TRADITION/ AFFILIATION	SPIRITUAL HEAD	Resident Teacher	City Centre	Country Centre	Regular Teachings	Meditation Facilities	Organized Retreats	Accommodation	Library	Bookshop	Newsletter
Conway Dzogchen Community, Conway, 20 Parsons Rd Conway, MA 01341. *Yantra yoga; Tibetan Medicine & astrology*		Tibetan: Dzogchen	Namkhai Norbu Rinpoche			•		•	•	•	•	•	•
Dharma Study Group, Firetower Rd, Falmouth, MA 02540. Until end 1984 c/o Marcelene Celiz, PO Box 144, Brewster, MA 02631	(617) 896 6233	Tibetan: Kagyu	Chogyam Trungpa Rinpoche	•		•	•	•	•	•	•	•	•
Insight Meditation Society, Pleasant St, Barre, MA 01005. *Resident tchr changes during the year; retreat centre in Vipassana tradition*	(617) 355 4378	Theravada				•		•	•				
Maha Siddha Nyingmapa, 53 Center St, Northampton MA 01060 (*Address provisional*)		Nyingma	Dodrup Chen Rinpoche				•	•			•		•
Northampton Dharmadhata, 25 Main St, Northampton MA 01060. *Psychology & other w/shops*	(413) 584 4880	Tibetan: Kagyu	Chogyam Trungpa Rinpoche		•		•	•			•		•
Sakya Center for Buddhist Studies and Meditation 5 Upland Rd 3, Cambridge MA 02140	(617) 492 5370	Tibetan	HH Sakya Trizin	•	•		•	•					
USA Michigan													
Ann Arbor Shim Gum Do Zen Group, 6 Geddes Hts, Ann Arbor, MI 48104. *Sword trg*	(313) 761 3770	Zen	Seung Sahn & Chang Sik Kim	•			•	•	•				
Karma Thegsum Chöling – Ann Arbor, 1033E University Apt 4, Ann Arbor, MI 4810. *Wang & Lung*	(313) 665 2065	Tibetan: Kagyu	Khenpo Karthar		•			•			•		•

NAME & ADDRESS	TELEPHONE	TRADITION/ AFFILIATION	SPIRITUAL HEAD	Resident Teacher	City Centre	Country Centre	Regular Teachings	Meditation Facilities	Organized Retreats	Accom-modation	Library	Bookshop	Newsletter
USA Missouri													
Kongosatta-In, Tendai Buddhist Mission, PO Box 212, Cape Girardeau, MO 63701. *Psychology & other w/shops*	(314) 334 1492	Tendai	Tendai Archbishop Jion Haba	•	•		•	•	•		•		•
USA New Hampshire													
Seacoast Region Dharma Study Group, Box 4, 35 Main St, Raymond, NH 03077	(603) 895 2674	Tibetan: Kagyu	Chogyam Trungpa Rinpoche					•					
USA New Jersey													
Mahayana Sutra and Tantra Center of New Jersey, 216a West Second St, Howell, NJ 07731. *Tibetan typesetting*	(201) 364 1824	Buddhist	Geshe Lobsang Tharchin	•		•	•	•	•	•	•	•	
Tashi Lhundo, 12 Kalmuk Rd, Howell, NJ 07731	(201) 363 6012	Tsong Khapa	Tenzing Dakpa	•		•		•		•			
USA New Mexico													
Alejandro Zendo, 397 Alejandro St, Santa Fe, NM 87501		Zen	Gentei Stewart		•			•					
Jemez Bodhi Mandala, PO Box 8, Jemez Springs, MN 87025. *Psychology & other w/shops; dance; tai chi; hot springs*	(505) 829 3854	Rinzai Zen	Joshu Sasaki			•	•	•	•	•	•	•	•
Karma Thegsum Chöling Retreat Center, PO Box 32, Puerto de Luna, NM 88432	(505) 472 3717	Tibetan	HH Gyalwa Karmapa			•		•	•	•	•	•	

NAME & ADDRESS	TELEPHONE	TRADITION/ AFFILIATION	SPIRITUAL HEAD	Resident Teacher	City Centre	Country Centre	Regular Teachings	Meditation Facilities	Organized Retreats	Accom-modation	Library	Bookshop	Newsletter
Lama Foundation, Box 240, San Cristobal, NM 87564 *Dance; tai chi; hermitages available*	(505) 586 0385	Tibetan, Zen, Vipassana				●	●	●	●	●	●	●	●
USA New York													
American Buddhist Academy, 331 Riverside Dr, New York. NY 10025, *Dance; tai chi; Japanese martial arts*	(212) 678 9213	Non sectarian (Ryukoku University)			●					●	●		
American Buddhist Movement, 9 301 W 45 St, New York. NY 10036. *Psychology & other w/shops; dance; tai chi*	(212) 489 1075	All traditions	Dr Kevin R O'Neil	●	●		●	●	●	●	●	●	●
Clear Mountain Zen Center, 8 School St, Chatham, New York. NY 12037		Zen	Rev Sogen Hart	●	●		●	●					
Dharma Study Group of Albany, 637 Morris St, Albany. NY 12208. *Psychology & other w/shops*	(518) 489 7358	Tibetan: Karma Kagyu	Chogyam Trungpa Rinpoche		●			●					
Grace Gratitude Buddhist Temple, 48 E Broadway, New York. NY 10002. *Sunday lunch*	(212) 925 1335	Ch'an	Hsu Yun	●	●		●	●	●		●		●
International Meditaion Center, 415 Franklin St, Buffalo, NY 14202	(716) 854 8195	Theravada	Anaganika Muninda						●				●
Ithaca Zen Center, 312 Auburn St, Ithaca, NY 14850 *Summer seminar on the Sutras*	(607) 273 3190	Zen	Rev Yoshin Radin	●	●			●					
Jacques Marchais Center of Tibetan Art, 338 Lighthouse Ave, Staten Island, NY 10306. *Museum; gardens; gift shop*	(212) 987 3478	Tibetan			●						●	●	●

NAME & ADDRESS	TELEPHONE	TRADITION/ AFFILIATION	SPIRITUAL HEAD	Resident Teacher	City Centre	Country Centre	Regular Teachings	Meditation Facilities	Organized Retreats	Accom- modation	Library	Bookshop	Newsletter
Jetsun Sakya, 623 West 129th St, New York. NY 10027. *Psychology & other w/shops*	(212) 222 8683	Tibetan: Sakya	HH Sakya Trizin	•	•		•	•	•		•	•	•
Karma Thegsun Chöling, 637 Washington Ave, Albany, NY 12206	(518) 489 2151	Tibetan: Karma Kagyu	HH Gyalwa Karmapa & Khenpo		•		•	•			•	•	•
Karma Thegsum Chöling, 412 West End Ave, Apt 5N, New York. NY 10024. *Tibetan language*	(212) 580 9282	Tibetan: Karma Kagyu	Khenpo Karthar Rinpoche		•		•	•			•	•	•
Karma Triyana Dharmachakra, 352 Mead Mountain Rd, Woodstock, NY 12498	(914) 679 2487	Tibetan: Kagyu	HH Gyalwa Karmapa			•	•	•	•	•		•	•
New York Buddhist Vihara, American Sri Lanka Buddhist Assocn Inc, 133-45 37th Ave, Flushing, NY 11354	(212) 445 1789	Theravada	Kurunegoda Piyatissa		•	•	•	•			•		
New York Zen Center of Rinzai-Ji, 6 Brewster Crt, Setuaket, NY 11733	(516) 751 8408	Zen		•	•		•	•	•		•	•	•
New York Zendo-Shobo-Ji, 223 E 67th St, New York, NY 10021. *Workshops*	(212) 861 3333	Zen	Eido Shimano Roshi	•	•		•	•	•				
Sung Bul Sa Temple and IBB TV Korean Buddhism – USA, 107 W 25th St, Apt 3D, New York, NY 10001. *Zen dance; Zen martial arts*	(212) 242 4792	Korean Buddhism	Abbot Do chul Pyo	•									
The Zen Center, 7 Arnold Park, Rochester, NY 14607	(716) 473 9180	Zen	Philip Kapleau Roshi	•	•		•	•	•		•	•	•
Zen Community of New York – Greyston Seminary, 690 W 247th St, Riverdale, NY 10471. *Inter-religious retreats; livelihoods; full-time trng prg; psychology & other w/shops*	(212) 543 5530	Mahayana	Bernard Tetsugen Glassman Sensei	•	•		•	•	•	•	•		•

NAME & ADDRESS	TELEPHONE	TRADITION/ AFFILIATION	SPIRITUAL HEAD	Resident Teacher	City Centre	Country Centre	Regular Teachings	Meditation Facilities	Organized Retreats	Accommodation	Library	Bookshop	Newsletter
Zen Mountain Center of New York, PO Box 197, NY 12457. *Psychology & other w/shops*	(914) 688 5914	Zen	Taizan Maizumi Roshi	●		●	●	●	●	●	●		●
USA North Carolina													
North Carolina Zen Center, Rt 1 Box 52, Pittsboro, NC 27312	(919) 542 4379	Zen											
USA Ohio													
Cleveland Buddhist Temple, 1573 E 214 St, Euclid, OH 44117. *Psychology & other w/shops*	(216) 692 1509	Mahayana	Rev Koshini Ogui, Sensei		●		●	●	●			●	●
Karma Thegsum Chöling, Columbus, 1078, Ravine Ridge Dr, Worthington, OH 43055	(614) 888 7549	Tibetan: Karma Kagyu	HH Gyalwa Karmapa	●				●			●	●	●
Lawrence Zen Center, 1115 Ohio St, Lawrence KS, OH 66044. *Poetry; reading*	(913) 842 7010	Chogye Zen	Zen Master Seung Sahn		●		●	●	●				
USA Oregon													
Buddha Root Farm, Rt 3, Box 186, OR 97467. *Oriental herb center*	(503) 271 2730	Mahayana	Master Hua			●		●					
Kagyu Changchub Chuling, 73 NE Monroe, Portland, OR 97212. *Tibetan language classes*	(503) 284 6697	Tibetan	Kalu Rinpoche	●	●		●	●	●		●	●	●

NAME & ADDRESS	TELEPHONE	TRADITION/ AFFILIATION	SPIRITUAL HEAD	Resident Teacher	City Centre	Country Centre	Regular Teachings	Meditation Facilities	Organized Retreats	Accommodation	Library	Bookshop	Newsletter
Oregon Zen Priory, 'The Portland Priory', 2237 NE 9th, Portland OR 97212	(503) 288 1467	Soto Zen	Master Jiyu-Kennett	●	●		●	●	●		●	●	●
Oregon Zen Priory, The Eugene Community Buddhist Church, 2255 Hilyard, Eugene, OR 97405	(503) 344 7377	Soto Zen	Master Jiyu-Kennett	●	●		●	●	●		●	●	●
USA Rhode Island													
Providence Zen Center, 528 Pound Rd, Cumberland RI 02864. *Psychology & other w/shops; 25 branch groups*	(401) 769 6464	Korean	Zen Master Seung Sahn	●		●	●	●	●	●	●	●	●
USA Texas													
Divine Awakening Library, 5708 Lexington, El Paso TX 79924	(915) 751 1508	Mahayana	Rex Winter		●			●			●		
Texas Zen Community, 226 E Austin St, Elgin, TX 78621. *Tofu factory*		Zen											
USA Vermont													
Dharma Study Group, Box 700, Pawlet, VT 05761. *Affiliate of Vajradhatu, Colorado*	(802) 325 3180	Tibetan: Kagyu	Chogyam Trungpa Rinpoche			●		●					
Karme-Chöling, Barnet, VT 05821. *Psychology & other w/shops; dance; tai chi; kyudo, ikebana; Dharma art*	(802) 633 2384	Tibetan: Kagyu	Chogyam Trungpa Rinpoche			●	●	●	●	●	●	●	
Milarepa Center, Barnet Mountain, Barnet, VT 05821	(802) 663 4136	Mahayana (FPMT)	Lama Yeshe & Zopa Rinpoche			●	●	●		●	●		

NAME & ADDRESS	TELEPHONE	TRADITION/ AFFILIATION	SPIRITUAL HEAD	Resident Teacher	City Centre	Country Centre	Regular Teachings	Meditation Facilities	Organized Retreats	Accommodation	Library	Bookshop	Newsletter
USA *Virginia*													
Blue Ridge Zen Group, 214 Rugby Rd, Charlottesville, VA 22903	(804) 973 5435	Zen (Rinzai)			●	●		●	●				
Ekoji Buddhist Temple, 8134 Old Keene Mill Rd; Springfield, VA 22152	(703) 569 2311	Mahayana	Jodo Shinshu	●	●		●	●			●		●
Rock Creek Buddhist Temple of America, Inc, 1823 N Lincoln St, Arlington, VA 22207	(703) 525 0909	Zen	Zenji Seikan Hasegawa		●			●		●			
USA *Washington*													
Bodhi-Dhamma Center, 8603-39th Ave, SW Seattle, WA 98136	(206) 932 1155	Mahayana	Tripitaka Master Hsuan Hua					●					
Seattle Zen Center, PO Box 5284 University Station, WA 98105	(206) 883 0487	Rinzai Zen	Takabayashi Genki Roshi	●	●	●	●	●	●		●	●	●
Tse Chen Kun Khab Choling, 2102 Dickinson, Olympia, WA 98502	(206) 754 7841	Vajrayana	Jigdal Dagchen Sakya Rinpoche	●	●		●	●			●		●
USA *Washington DC*													
The Mahayana Sutra and Tantra Center, PO Box 23102, L'Enfant Plaza Stn, Washington DC 20024 *Biweekly tsechu ceremonies; translation & publications; monastic aid, children's Buddhist class*	(301) 585 4575	Mahayana	Geshe Lobsang Tharchin	●	●				●		●		

NAME & ADDRESS	TELEPHONE	TRADITION/ AFFILIATION	SPIRITUAL HEAD	Resident Teacher	City Centre	Country Centre	Regular Teachings	Meditation Facilities	Organized Retreats	Accommodation	Library	Bookshop	Newsletter
Newsletter for North American Buddhist Women, c/o Karen Gray, 825 New Hampshire Ave NW, 304, Washington DC 20037	(202) 333 6947	All traditions							•		•	•	
USA Wisconsin													
Deer Park, PO Box 5366, Madison, WI 53705. *Monastery: plg for accommodation in progress*	(608) 835 5572	Tibetan	Geshe Sopa		•		•	•			•		•
Milwaukee Dharmadhatu, 1810 E North Ave, Milwaukee, WI 53211	(414) 276 8005	Tibetan	Chogyam Trungpa Rinpoche	•	•		•	•				•	
YUGOSLAVIA													
Nongokata Dojo, Lenjinova 23, 52000 Pula. *Kempo; Chinese yoga*		Shingon (Chinese)	Shifu Nagaboshi Tomio	•		•	•	•	•				•
ZAMBIA													
Buddhist Society of Zambia, PO Box 21972, Kitwe	Kitwe 216996	Hinayana (Sri Lanka)	Malwatte Maha-nayake Kandy	•			•		•		•		•

Part Two
Unconfirmed Addresses

ARGENTINA

Ing. Mariano Moriera, Higgins 3440, 1429 Buenos Aires.

AUSTRALIA *ACT*

Buddhist Society of ACT, PO Box 1149, Canberra City, ACT 2600.
Canberra Buddhist Society, Garran Hall, ANU, Box 3, Canberra City, ACT 2601.

AUSTRALIA *NSW*

Australia K.K. Trust, PO Box 1864, Sydney, NSW 2001.
Australian/Chinese Buddhist Society, C/- Mr Sykham, PO Box 45, Canley Heights, NSW 2166.
Banksia Institute, 26 Corfe Street, Redrock, NSW 2452.
Australian Buddhist Vihara, 1 Third Avenue, North Katoomba, NSW 2780.
Buddhadamma Society of Sydney, 88 Stanmore Road, Stanmore, NSW 2048.
Buddha Sanana Society of NSW, PO Box 650, North Sydney, NSW 2060.
The Buddhist Family, 69 Jersey Road, Woolhara, NSW 2025.
The Buddhist Society of NSW, Villa 7, 24 Garden Street, East Lakes, PO Box 1489, Sydney, NSW.
Chinese Buddhist Society, 54 Dixon Street, Haymarket, Sydney, NSW 2000. Phone: (02) 212 3666.
Dhamma House, 506 Wilson Street, Chippendale, NSW 2008.
Dhamma Talks & Meditation Sessions, 1 Tilopea Street, Wollestonecraft, NSW 2065.

Kargyu Do Ngak·Cho Ling, 16 Slade Avenue, Lindfield, NSW 2070. Phone: (02) 46 1256.
Karma Tashi Choling Sanctuary, C/- Margaret Martin, Wyndham PO via Bega, NSW 2550.
Kwan Yin Dhyana Temple, 117 Albion Street, Surry Hills, NSW 2010.
Laotian Buddhist Society, C/- Mr Vitaisarn, 26 Arlewis Street, Chester Hill, NSW 2162.
Loden Mahayana Centre, 175 Denison Street, Dulwich Hill, NSW 2203. Phone: (02) 569 0918.
Maha Makut Foundation, 9 Ripon Way, Rosebery, NSW 2018.
Metta Foundation, 2 Wellington Street, Bondi, NSW 2026. Phone: (02) 309 1419.
Nichiren Shoshu of Australia, 107 Perouse Street, Randwick, NSW 2031.
North Sydney Buddhist Society, 144 Walker Street, North Sydney, NSW 2060. Phone: (02) 929 8643.
Nyingma Society for Buddhist Studies, Yankee Creek, Box 257 Mullumbimby, NSW 2482.
Sydney Zen Group, 7 Provincial Road, Lindfield, NSW 2070. Phone: (02) 46 5316.
Vietnamese Buddhist Society of NSW, 1 Ridgewell Street, Lakemba, NSW 2195. Phone: (02) 759 0170.
Vipassana Contact Centre, C/- M & A Dowling, 506 Wilson Street, Chippendale, NSW 2008. Phone: (02) 698 9181.
Vipassana Information, PO Box 1685, North Sydney, NSW 2060. Phone: (02) 799 7113.
Vipassana Meditation Centre, PO Box 103, Blackheath, NSW 2785.

AUSTRALIA *Queensland*

Buddhist Society, C/-D Jayasinghe Vedagedera, 38 Ross River Road, Muddingburra, QLD 4812.

Nichiren Shosho of Australia, 30 Mackenzie Street, Manly West, QLD 4179. Phone: (07) 394 2848.

Vipassana Information, C/-R & M Peters, Pinaroo, Browns Creek Road, Eumundi, QLD 4562.

Zen Buddhist Retreat, Service Creek Road, Evelyn Central, QLD 4872.

AUSTRALIA *South Australia*

Buddhist Association of SA, PO Box 48, Walkerville, SA 5081.

Buddha House, PO Box 93, Eastwood, SA 5063.

Dharma Study Group, 65 Stanby Street, North Adelaide, SA 5006.

Victory Centre, PO Box 481, North Adelaide, SA 5006.

Vipassana Information, C/-M Tothill, 29 Williams Avenue, Hackham West, SA 5163.

AUSTRALIA *Victoria*

Buddhist Federation of Australia, PO Box 2568W, Melbourne, VIC 3000.

Buddhist House, 226 Mary Street, Richmond, VIC 3121.

Dai Bi Quan Am, 8 Prince Street, Footscray, VIC 3011. Phone: (03) 317 7416.

Dhamma House, 13 Coonhil Crescent, Malvern, VIC 3144. Phone: (03) 509 9426.

Karma Kagyu, Ewan Chokor Ling, 11 Selbourne Road, Kew, VIC 3101.

La Trobe Buddhist Society, La Trobe University, Plenty Road, Bundoora, VIC 3083. Phone: (03) 479 2849.

Loden Ganden Mahayana Centre, 178 George Street, East Melbourne, VIC 3002.

Melbourne Zen Group, 2 Park Parade, North Fitzroy, VIC 3068.

Nichiren Shoshu Sokagakkai of Australia, 5 Medhurst Street, East Burwood, VIC 3125.

RMIT Buddhist Society, PO Box 247, (Cnr Swanston & Latrobe Streets), Melbourne, VIC 3000.

Satsuma Dojo Zen Centre, 14 Orient Avenue, Mitcham, VIC 3132. Phone: (03) 874 3537.

Vietnamese Buddhist Association of Victoria, 17 Hoddle Street, Richmond, VIC 3121.

Vipassana Information, C/- M & T Barnes, 3 Carrington Grove, East St Kilda, VIC 3182. Phone: (03) 527 6889.

AUSTRIA

Buddha Dharma Zentrum, C/- Andrea Seabury Lake, Franchstrasse 31, 8010 Graz.

Buddhistische Gemeinschaft, Merianstrasse, 5020 Salzburg. Phone: (06222) 79 08 52.

Buddhistische Gemeinschaft Wien, Dannebergplatz 10, 1030 Vienna. Phone: (0222) 726 06 45.

Bund Für Neue Lebensform, Lehargasse 1, 1060 Vienna. Phone: (0222) 574 80 34.

Institut Für Tibetologie, Maria Thereienstrasse 3, 1090 Vienna.

Karpa De Phel Ling, C/- Thule G-Jug, Kastellfeldgasse 17, 8010 Graz.

Karma Namgyal Ling, C/- E Skrleta, Octopus Verlag, Postfach 53, 1236 Vienna.

Nyingmapa Meditation Centre, C/- M De Bernard, Drof 19/13, 6323 Bad Haring.

Österreichische Buddhistische Union, Postfach, 1236 Vienna. Phone: (06222) 79 08 52.

Shitennoji Buddistisches Kulturzentrum Österreich, Kroffel Steigstrasse 32, 2371 Hinterbrühl.

Vienna Dharmadhatu, Fleischmarkt 16, 1010 Vienna. Phone: 52 71 46.
Verein Der Freunde des Buddh. Kultur & Meditations Zentrum, Postfach 53, 1236 Scheibbs.

BANGLADESH

Aggameda Buddhist Temple, Cox's Bazaar, Chittagong.
Bangladesh Bauddha Kristi Prachar Sangha Dharmmara Jika, Buddhist Monastery, Kamalapur, Dacca 14.
Bangladesh Buddha Samiti, Buddhist Monastery, Buddhist Temple Road, Chittagong.
Bangladesh Buddhist Youth Council, 20 Jigatola, Dacca 9.
Bangladesh Buddhist Youth Federation, 80A Santinager, Dacca 2.
Buddhist Temple, Ramu.
Chittagong Buddhist Monastery, Nanderakaman, Buddhist Temple Road, Chittagong.
Mir Zapur Santdham Vihar, PO 2 Vill Mirgapur, Hatazari, Chittagong.
Padua Buddhist Temple, Satkania, Chittagong.

BELGIUM

Belgian Buddhist Assoc., 8 Avenue De La Charmille, Box 16, 1200 Brussels.
Buddhist Study Centre of Belgium, 74 Rue De L'Orient, Brussels.
Buddhist Study Centre, C/- R Kiere, 64 Rue Branche, Ans (Liege).
Centre Bouddique Soto Zen de Belgique, Avenue Du Capricorne 143, 1200 Brussels. Phone: 771 59 47.

Centres Bouddhiques Ljan'na, Rue Ed Van Camvenbergh 16, 1020 Brussels.
Institut Belge Des Hautes Etudes Bouddhiques, Chaussee De Louvain 696, 1030 Brussels.
Karma Jonam Gyamtso Ling, Grote Nonstraat 36, 2000 Antwerp.
Karma Samten Ling, Vijphoekstraat 19, 2600 Berchen.
Karma Shedrup Ling, Karma Kagyu Institute, 33 Rue Capouillet, 1060 Brussels. Phone: (2) 537 54 07.
Karma Sonam Gyamtso Ling, Grote Hondstraat 36, 2000 Antwerp. Phone: (3) 139 61 55.
Orgen Kunzang Choling, La Domaine De La Claire, 111-113 Rue de Lovourne, 1050 Brussels. Phone: 648 14 07.
Torben Rosgaard, Kelin Waverstraat 50, 3054 Loonbeek.

BHUTAN

Paro Kitchu Monastery, Paro.

BRAZIL

Brasilia Karma Thegsum Choling, c/o Jacira Brandao da Silva, SQS 307 – BLC Apt 111, 70 – 354, Brasilia DF.
Federacao das Sietas Buddhistas do Brasil, Avenida Paulo Ferreira 1133, Piqueri S Paulo.
Fundacao Educacional e Cultural Yehan Numata, A/C Mitutoyo do Brasil Industria e Comercio LTDA, Rua Brigadeiro Galvao, 109 Barra Funda, Caixa Postal 4225, CEP – 01151, Sao Paulo (SP).
Sociedade Budista do Brasil, Estrada Dom Joaquim Mamede 45, Sta.., Tereza Rio de Janeiro.

BURMA

The Buddhist Discussion Group, The Soni Building, 'C' Road Mandalay.

Buddha Sasawa Council Press, Kaba-Aye PO, Rangoon.

Centre for Advanced Buddhist Studies, Kaba Aye Pagoda, Rangoon.

Chittagong Buddhist Association, 158 Upper Phayre Street, Kandawglay, Rangoon.

International Meditation Centre, Sayama & UC Tin, 31A Inya Myaing Road, University Post Office, Rangoon.

Sein Young Chi Pagoda, Shewedagon Pagoda Road, Rangoon.

CAMBODIA

Botum Vaddei Pagoda, Phnon Penh.

Buddhist Association Khmer Republic, Wat Unna Lom, Phnon Penh.

Lanka Vihare, Phnon Penh.

Onalom Pagoda, Phnon Penh.

Phnon Penh Pagoda, Phnon Penh.

Silver Temple, Phnon Penh.

Wat Pothiveal Pagoda, Battambang.

CANADA *Alberta*

Edmonton Dharma Study Group, 11526 77th Avenue, Edmonton, Alberta T6G OM1.

Honpa Buddhist Church of Alberta, Box 286, Raymond, Alberta.

Karma Kagyu Centre, 126 8th Avenue SE, Calgary, Alberta T2P 4KI.

Marpa Gompa Meditation Society, 1346 Frentenac Avenue SW, Calgary, Alberta T2T 1B8.

CANADA *British Columbia*

Bodhi Dharma Society, 7011 Marguerite Street, Vancouver BC.

Buddhayana Educational Association, 3813 West 21st Avenue, Vancouver BC.

Crystal Mountain, PO Box 69767, Station K, Vancouver BC.

Dharmadhatu, 3285 Heather Street, Vancouver BC, 4S2 3KY.

Gaden Rime Zongling, 720 West 27th Avenue, Vancouver BC V5Z 2G6.

Jetsun Chimmy Luding, 7340 Forbisher Drive, Richmond, British Columbia V7C 4N5. Phone: (604) 271 7423.

Kagyu Kunchab Choling, 725 W 14th Street, Vancouver BC.

Kagyu Kunkhyab Choling, 4941 Sidley Street, Burnaby, British Columbia.

Kelowan Buddhist Church, 1065 Borden Avenue, Kelowan, British Columbia.

Sakya Bodhi Dharma Society, 7340 Frobisher Drive, Richmond, Vancouver BC V7C 4N5.

Sakya Thubten Kunga Choeling, 1149 Leonard Street, Victoria BC V8V 2S3. Phone: (604) 385 4828.

Universal Buddhist Temple, 525 49th Avenue, Vancouver V5W 2H1.

Vancouver Dharmadhatu, 3285 Heather Street, Vancouver BC V5Z 1X2. Phone: (604) 874 8420.

Vancouver Dhamma House, 2670 West Second Avenue, Vancoucer BC. Phone: (604) 734 9444.

CANADA *Manitoba*

Manitoba Buddhist Association, 825 Winnipeg 3, Manitoba.

CANADA *Nova Scotia*

Dharmadhatu, Box 2002 Station M, Halifax, Nova Scotia B3J 3B7.
Mahayana Buddhist Society, PO Box 302, Nova Scotia B0P IR0.

CANADA *Ontario*

Buddhist Circle of Ottawa, Box 2573, Station D, Ottawa, Ontario.
The Buddhist Churches of Canada, 918 Bathurst Street, Toronto, Ontario.
Campo Gangara Wang du Ling, 1290 Dorchester Avenue, Ottawa, Ontario K1Z 8E7.
Crystal Staff, 42 Carlyle Avenue, Ottawa, Ontario K1S 4T4.
Kampo Gangra Drubgyud Ling, 200 Balsam Avenue, Toronto, Ontario M4E 3C3. Phone: (416) 699 3801.
Karma Kagyu Centre, C/- C Peterson, 8 Everingham Court, Willowdale, Ontario M2M 2J5.
Karma Kagyu Society, PO Box 5399, Station A, Toronto, Ontario M5W 1N6. Phone: (416) 763 2103.
Karma Tilo Chompheling, 834 Windemere Avenue, Toronto, Ontario M6S 3M6. Phone: (416) 767 4513.
Kitchener-Waterloo Dharma Study Group, 70 Zeller Street, Kitchener, Ontario N2G 3W6. Phone: (519) 893 9595.
Ontario Dharma Study Group, Box 101, Peterborough, Ontario.
Ontario Zen Centre, 1 Hambly Avenue, Toronto, Ontario M4E 2R5. Phone: (416) 691 0592.

Ottawa Buddhist Association, 26 Rich Little Drive, Ottawa, Ontario.
Ottawa Forming Dharmadhatu, 158 Russell Avenue, Ottawa, Ontario KIN 7X4. Phone: (613) 232 3350.
Samten Gatsel Ling, 528 Sydney Street, Belleville, Ontario.
Sun Lotus Society, 378 Markham Street, Apt. B-1, Toronto, Ontario M6G 2K9.
Tibet Centre, 26 Spencer Street, Toronto, Ontario.
Toronto Dharmadhatu, 103 Church Street, Toronto, Ontario M5C 2G3. Phone: (416) 535 5882.
Toronto Mahavihara Society, 3595 Kingston Road, Scarborough, Ontario MIM IR8.
Toronto Zen Centre, 569 Christie Street, Toronto, Ontario M6G 3E4.
Tsan Shan Vihara, 5 Longwood Drive, Dom Mills, Ontario.
Vietnamese Canadian Buddhist Association, Box 6795, Ottaway, Ontario K2A 3Z4.

CANADA *Quebec*

Gosselin, Roger, 189 Rue St Jacques, East Angus, PQ JOB IRO Quebec. Phone: (819) 872 3368.
Kuan-Yin Buddhist Society, 2537 Rue Frontenac 6, Montreal, Quebec H2K 3A2. Phone: (514) 525 3791.
Lien Hoa Temple, 715 Provencher Boulevard, Brossard, Quebec J4W IY4. Phone: (514) 672 7948.
Montreal Buddhist Church, 5250 St True Urbain Street, Montreal, Quebec, Canada.
Montreal Dharmadhatu, 1534 Pine Avenue West, Montreal, Quebec H3Q IB4.
Montreal Zen Centre, 824 Park Stanley, Ahunstic, Quebec. Phone: (514) 388 4518.

Pagode Bouddhique Chua, 4450 Van Horne, Montreal, Quebec H3S ISI. Phone: (514) 733 3841.

CANADA *Saskatchewan*

Crystal Tree, C/- La Point, 613 Albert Avenue, Seakatoon, Saskatchewan.

CANADA *Yukon*

Awareness Centre, 2 Redwood, White Horse, Yukon YIA 4B3.
Karma Kagyu Centre, PO Box 4939, Whitehorse, Yukon Territory YIA 4S2.

CHINA

Buddhist Association of China, 11 Yangshi Da Jie, Peking.

COLUMBIA

San Cristobal KTC (Karma Thegsum Choling) Carrera 2 Calle 1, Gra. Hilomar, Ambrozio Plaza, San Cristobal.

CZECHOSLOVAKIA

Dr Dusan Kafka, Anenska 5/186, Stare Mesto, Praha 1.

DENMARK

Copenhagen Dharma Study Group, 2720 Vanlose, Randbol 1EJ8, Copenhagen. Phone: (01) 747 22 90.
Hesbjergs Ravada Buddhist Education & Meditation Centre, Hesbjersvag 50, 5491 Blommonslyst, Fyn.
Kargyu Centre for Tibetan Buddhism, Skindergarde 5, 1159 Copenhagen.
Karma Chopel Ling, Vejlebyvej 16, 4970 Rodby.
Karma Geleg Tardje Ling, C/- F Ryborg, Rugaardsvej 109, 5000 Odense.
Karma Tjo Pael Ling, Retreat Centre, Dueholm, Korterupvei 21, 4920 Sollested.

FINLAND

Buddhism Yatavat, Friends of Buddhism in Finland, Ulvilante 29/2 E 81, 00350 Helsinki 35.
Finnish Buddhist Association FWBO, Upasika Sumati, Alberti Kayu, 00100 Helsinki.
Karma Gyalwai Shjing, C/- Lahdenmaki, 00250 Helsinki. Phone: (90) 616 0324.
Lansimainsen Buddhalaisen, Veljeskunnan Ystavat FWBO. 00120 Helsinki 12.

FRANCE

Association Bouddhique Franco - Vietnamienne, 575 Boulevard De Balzac, Saint Aygulf, 83600 Frejus.
Association Bouddhiste Thar Den Ling, 207 Rue St Maur, 75010 Paris.

Association Bouddhiste Thar Den Ling, 146 Rue Perronet, 92200 Neuilly.

Association Culturelle Bouddique Linh-So'n, 9 Avenue Jean-Jaurés, 94340 Joinville-le-Pont.

Association Culturelle Des Bouddhistes de France, Delegation Du Lot-et Garonne, 15 Rue Claude Debussy, 47300 Villeneuve Sur Lot. Phone: (58) 70 27 86.

Association Culturelle Bouddhique De Marseille, 3 Rue de la Pagode, 13015 Marseille.

Associationes Des Bouddhistes Vietnamiens en France, 2 Square Des Mimosas, 75013 Paris. Phone: 558 61 87.

Association Dorje Nyingpo, 25 Rue Pradier, 75019 Paris.

Association Groupe Yoga, Colette Mauchamps, 5 Rue De la Liberte, 21000 Dijon.

Association Zen D'Europe, 46 Rue Pernety, 75014 Paris. Phone: 724 56 89.

Association Zen D'Occident, 45 Rue Des Valles, 91800 Brundy.

Bodhinyanarama Monastere, 6 Chemin De Boucharin, 07300 Tournon-S-Rhone.

Le Bodhisat (Revue), Mme Stork, 90 Boulevard Du Montparnasse, 75014 Paris.

Buddhist Union of Europe, 5 Chemin Du Mont Gros, 06500 Menton.

Les Cahiers Du Bouddhisme, 3 Boulevard De La Saussaye, 92200 Neuilly/Seine.

Centre Bouddhiste Ngor-E-Wam Kunzang-Ling, 8 Cour Saint Pierre, 75017 Paris. Phone: (1) 353 26 40.

Centre Bouddhiste Tibetan, 347 Rue De Paradis, 13008 Marseille.

Centre Bouddhique Tibetan, Rue De Tresoiries De La Bourse, 3400 Montpellier.

Centre Bouddhiste Tibetain, 227/261 Promenade Des Anglais, 06220 Nice.

Centre Bouddhiste Tibetain, (Guepel Tchantchoup Ling), 107 Avenue Flouquet, 94240 L'Hay-Les-Roses. Phone: (1) 350 83 49.

Centre Bouddhiste Tibetain Yiga Tcheudzin, 27 Avenue Du Marechal-Juin, 04000 Digne. Phone: (92) 31 32 38.

Centre Bouddhique Vajrayana Kagyu Dzong, 24 Rue Phillipe Hecht, 75019 Paris. Phone: 205 24 78.

Centre De Meditation, C/- Gervias, 2 Rue de Brea, 44000 Nantes.

Centre De Meditation, C/- Alain Taubert, 27 Route de Rosheim, 67530 Boersch.

Centre de Normandie, C/- M. & Mme. Franck, Lamalefendiere, St Georges De Livaye, 50370 Brecey.

Centre D'Etudes Bouddhiques De Sri Lanka, 51 Rue Barbes, 92120 Mont Rouge.

Centre D'Etude Des Medicines Douces, 35 Chemin Du Gigot, 91100 Saintry. Phone: (6) 075 54 68.

Centre D'Etude De La Tradition et de la Culture Tibetain, 5 Residence de la Pierrerie, 77680 Roissy en France.

Centre D'Etudes Bouddhiques de Gretz, Gretz, 77220 Tournan.

Centre Ewan Ohende Ling, Les Ventes, 27930 Evreux. Phone: (32) 37 42 05.

Centre Francais de la Pali Bouddhistes Union, 6 Avenue Pierre Denave, 71000 Macon.

Centre Regional Francais de L'Association Mondaile des Bouddhistes, 90 Boulevard Montparnasse, 75014 Paris. Phone: 326 53 19.

Centre Tibetain, 10 Avenue Victor Hugo, Tourne Feville, 31100 Toulouse.

Centre Tibetain Yiga Tcheudzin, C/- G Driessens, Boisset et Gaujac, 30140 Anduze.

Centre Zen Du Taille, Veseaux, 07200 Aubenas.

Chartreuse de St Hugon, Arvillard, 73110 La Rochette.

La Communaute Bouddhique De France, 40 Rue de Ranelagh, 75018 Paris.

Dagpo Kagyu Ling, La Sonnerie, St Leon Sur Vezere, Landrevie, 24290 Montignac, Dordogne.

Daychen Jong, C/- Ann Berry, 76 Rue La Courbe, 75015 Paris.

Dojo Zen, 6 Rue Brulee, 67000 Strasbourg.

Dorjea Nyingpo, 22 Rue Burq, 75018 Paris.

Ewam Sangupa Ling, C/- Mme Languillon, 145 Rue du Fbg St Denis, 75010 Paris.

Ewam Phende Ling, 27930 Les Ventes-Evereux.

Federation Des Bouddhistes de France, 27 Rue Saint Dominique, 75007 Paris.

French Regional Centre of WFB, 98 Chemin de la Calade, 06250 Mougins.

Groupe D'Etude Du Dharma, 2 Square du Roule, 75008 Paris.

Groupement Bouddhiste, 7 Rue Jean Dagneaux, 71000 Macon.

Hoi Phak Tu Wiek'Nam Tai Phag, Pagode Truc Lam, 9 Rue de Neuchatel 9, 91120 Villebon Sur Yvette.

Institut International Bouddhique, M. Jean Ober, 1 Villa Boissiere, 75016 Paris. Phone: 627 68 81.

International Zen Association, 46 Rue Pernety, 75014 Paris.

Kagyu Detchen Tcheu Ling, 210 Rue D'Entraigues, 37000 Tours. Phone: (47) 20 84 85.

Kagyu Dzong, C/- M. Francois, 6 Avenue de Liege, 94160 Saint Mande. Phone: (1) 328 88 88.

Kagyu Dzong, C/- Francis Juiff, 5 Rue Henri Brissou, 75018 Paris.

Kagyu Dzong, Flat 8, 2 Rue Sadie le Conte, 75019 Paris. Phone: 205 24 78.

Kagyu Dzong, 70 Rue Gagnee, 94400 Vitry Sur Seine.

Kagyu Ling C'Ebouddhiste Vajrayana, Chateau de Plaige, La Boulaye, 71320 Toulon Sur Arroux. Phone: (85) 79 43 41.

Kagyu Rintchen Tscheu Ling, C/- Mme. Dany Guelton, Secretariat, Mas De Balmes, 34970 Lattes.

Kagyu Vajradhara Ling, Domaine Du Chateau D'Osmont, Aubry le Panthou, 61120 Vimoutiers.

Karma Doupjou Peljeling, 10 Ave Victor Hugo, 31170 Toune Feuille Toulouse.

Karma Kagyu Centre, Mme Franc, 6 Brud de Roeilly, 75012 Paris. Phone: (01) 340 98 36.

Karma Khechog Tsangpo, Dr George Allyn, 29 Rue Wilhelm, Paris. 16E. Phone: 236 31 33.

Karma Puntso Tcheuling, C/- M Honorat, 4 Rue Victor Leyolet, 13100 Aix-En-Provence.

Karma Samten Choling, Les Tranchats, 24580 Plazac, Rouffignac, Dordogne.

Karma Thisum Choling, 5 Rue Reydie, 2400 Perigeux.

Monastere Du Taille, Vesseaux, 07200 Aubenas.

Monastere Bodhinya Narama, 6 Chemin de Boucharin, 67300 Touron.

Monastere Bouddhique de la Maha Prajnaparamita, Avenue des Bouleaux, 77880 Gretz.

Nenang Samten Choling, Les Tranchats, 24580 Plazac par Rouffignac.

Nichiren Shoshu Francais et Sokagakkai, 4 Rue Gachelin, 92330 Sceaux. Phone: 1176.

Nihonzan Myohoji, 38 Rue Polonbeau, Paris 18E.

Nyima Dzong, Chateau des Soleils, 04120 Castellane.

Nyima Dzong Monastery, Domain Ogyen Kunzang, Claire Lumiere, Pont de Solells, Georges du Verdon-04.

Order of Western Anagarakas, Rene Joly le Goth Rosieres, 43800 Vorey Sur Arton.

Orgyen Samye Choling, 'Langerol', St Leon-Sur-Vezere, 24290 Montignac. Phone: (53) 50 75 29.

Pagode de Vincennes, 40 Route Circulaire du Lac Daumesnil, 75012 Paris.

Pagode Khanh Anh, Avenue Henri Barbusse 14, 92220 Bagneux. Phone: 655 84 44.

Rigpa, C/- D Muhlebach, 41 Rue Grande, Mallemort, 13370 Aix. Phone: (90) 57 42 52.

Sadhana, 95 Boulevard Magenta, 75010 Paris.

Sakya Ling, 21 Rue de L'Observatoire, 67000 Strassbourg.

Sakya Tsechen Ling, Institut de Bouddhisme Tibetain, 5 Rond Point du Vignoble, 67520 Marlenheim, Kuttolsheim.

Jean Claude See, 52 Rue de Verneuil, 57007 Paris. Phone: (1) 261 16 44.

Societe des Amis du Bouddhisme, 4 Square Rapp, 75007 Paris. Phone: 551 81 25.

Tardeu Ling, 37 Rue David d'Angers, 75019 Paris.

Temple Bouddique De Paris, Bois De Vincennes, Paris.

Temple Bouddhiste Zen, 98 Chemin de la Calade, 06 Mougins. Phone: 90 14 78.

Temple Nihonzan Myohoji, 38 Rue Polonceau, 75018 Paris.

That Due Ling, 46 Rue Perronet, 92200 Rouilly Sur Seine.

World Fellowship of Buddhists French Regional Centre, 06250 Mougins.

Zen Centre, M Taponier, Le Près Lambin, 74 Air Julie en Genevoi.

Zen Centre, C/- Guetault, 2 Rue Fleurie, 37 St Cyrs Loire, Tours.

GERMANY

Akademisches Auslandsamt, C/- Guenter Valentin, Burgstr 6, 6301 Wettenberg 1.

Amitabha Buddha Sangha, Heinz Schmitter, Hauptstr 81, 5591 Landerkern.

Buddhistische Assoziation Bonn, Frau Haussels, Aggerstr 10, 5300 Bonn 2.

Buddhistische Gemeinde am Niederrhein, Wilhelm Mueller, Lindenstr 41, 4130 Moers 1.

Buddhistische Gemeinschaft Jodo Shin, c/o G Kell, Coubierestr 8 1000 Berlin 30. Phone: (030) 21 91 13.

Buddhistische Gemeinschaft Jodo Shin, Gerd-Dieter Minor, Simmernerstr 88a. 5400 Koblenz 1.

Buddhistische Gemeinschaft Mannheim, Friedhelm Kohler, T6 30, 6800 Mannheim.

Buddhistische Gesellschaft Berlin e.V. Dr Bodo Angermann, Seestr 12, 1000 Berlin 28. Phone: 404 38 38.

Buddhistische Gesellschaft Hamburg e.V., Beisserstr 23, 2000 Hamburg 63. Phone: 631 36 96.

Buddhistische Gesellschaft Muenchen, c/o Gunter Schopfer, Schleissheimerstr 205A, 8000 Muenchen 40. Phone: (089) 31 68 16.

Buddhistischer Amida Tempel, Bundesplatz 17, 1000 Berlin 31.

Buddhistischer Arbeitskreis Bodensee, Dr Med H K Gottmann, Obere St Leonhardstr 70, 7770 Uberlingen. Phone: (07551) 65206.

Buddhistischer Kreis, Frau Anneliese Sump, Bennigsenstr 68B, 2800 Bremen. Phone: (0421) 44 04 80.

Buddhistischer Kreis Chagpori, Ludwig Schafft, Sonnenhang 14, 8069 Ilmmuenster.

Buddhistischer Kreis Landshut, Angelika Simmet, Gollweg 4, 8300 Landshut.

Buddhistischer Kreis Stuttgart, Stumpenhof 23, 7310 Plochingen. Phone: (08153) 21086.

Buddhistischer Tempel, Rubinstr 14, 8000 Muenchen, Contact Address: Uwe Hartman, Wolfrashausener Str 294 b, 8000 Muenchen 71.

Buddhistisches Astrologisches, Zentrum Manjushri Mandala, Nuenninweg 150, 4400 Muenster.

Buddhistisches Haus, Edelhofdam 54, 1000 Berlin 28. Phone: (030) 401 17 84.

Buddhistisches Haus, Georg Grimm, 8919 Utting A/Ammersee. Phone: (08806) 7507.

Buddhistisches Seminar, Paul Debes, Katzeneichen 6, 8581 Bindlach-Benk.

Buddhistisches Seminar, Im Oberdorf 32, 7763 Ohningen 3.

Buddhist Promoting Foundation, c/o Sampoh, Messgeraete Vertriebs-Gesellschaft, Borsigstr 8-10, 4040 Neuss 21.

Dharma-Haus Vogelsberg, Vajradhatu Europa Pakshi Ling, Kirchweg 5, 6315 Muecke 1. Phone: 64 00 17 47.

Dharma-Studien-Gruppe, Dr E Pagenstecher, Nerotal 77, 6200 Wiesbaden. Phone: 52 3929.

Dharma-Studien-Gruppe, Gerhard Rohlsstr 24, 5300 Bonn 2. Phone: (0228) 35 28 28.

Dharma-Studien-Gruppe Muenchen, Schirmerweg 90, 8000 Muenchen 60. Phone: 811 68 99.

Drikung Dharmatara Ling, c/o Gertrud Zovkic, Rathelbeckstr 289-4, 4000 Dusseldorf 12. Phone: (0211) 20 12 58.

Drikung Nga Dan Choling Gemein. Verein fur Tibetischen, Medelon 21, 5789 Medebach/Sauerland.

Freie Buddhistische Arbeitsgemeinschaft Leverkusen, c/o Dr Kruckenberg, Berta-von-Suttnersstr 59, 5090 Leverkusen 1. Phone: (0214) 46373.

Freunde des Westlichen Buddhistischen Ordens, Dhammaloka und Dharmapriya, Rechtstr 9, 4300 Essen 11. Phone: (0201) 68 29 79.

Haus der Stille e.V., Muehlenweg 20, 2059 Roseburg u/Buechen, Germany. Phone: (0415) 8214.

Gespraechskreis, Herbert P. Debes, Gabelsberger Str 48, 6050 Offenbach. Phone: (0611) 83 49 84.

Gespraechs-und Meditations Kreis, Reino Kropfgans, Hardtplaetzchen 63, 5600 Wuppertal 23.

Kamalasila Institute for Buddhist Studies, Schloss Wachendorf, 5353 Mechernich-Wachendorf. Phone: (02256) 7168.

Karma Chang Chub Choe Phel Ling, c/o Dorothea Nett, Gaisberstr 27, 6900 Heidelberg. Phone: (06221) 16 09 17.

Karma Dagpo Drub Djy Choe Khor Ling, Holunderstr 116, 2800 Bremen 1.

Karma Dhagpo Gyurme Ling, c/o Barbara Schmale, Blutenburgerstr 90, 8000 Muenchen 19. Phone: (089) 129 93 22.

Karma Dhagpo Gyurme Ling, c/o Wolfgang Neugebauer, Landwehrstr 83, 8000 Muenchen 2. Phone: (089) 53 39 00.

Karma Dechen Oeser Ling, c/o Rainer Prochnow, Magnitorwall 10, 3300 Braunschweig. Phone: (0531) 4 31 66.

Karma Drub Djy Ling, An der Verbindungsbahn 10, 2000 Hamburg 13. Phone: 410 60 08.

Karma Drub Djy Puntshok, c/o H Giller & D Zache, Werderstr 50, 7500 Karlsruhe. Phone: (0721) 32773.

Karma Drub Gyue Thektschen Ling, *Contact address:* Hans-Harald Niemeyer, Gitteweg 5, 7801 Bollschweil. Phone: (07633) 88 27.

Karma Gyalsten Ling, c/o Fremy, H Christophers, Olde Husen 2, 2944 Wittmund 4.

Karma Gyurmed Ling, c/o Sieglinde Schemann, Ledderhosenweg, 6500 Bad Kreuznach. Phone: (0671) 69336.

Karma Gyurme Gyamtso Ling, c/o J. Trettin, Muellerstr 145, 1000 Berlin 65. Phone: (030) 462 49 21.

Karma Kagyu Ling, c/o G Wick, Wiesenstr 25, 5810 Witten. Phone: (02302) 53 052.

Karma Kagyu Ling, c/o C Becker, Schulplatz 12, 4133 Neukirchenvluyn.

Karma Phuntsok Gephel Ling, c/o Galas, Kleingartenweg 15, 8900 Augsburg 21. Phone: (0821) 8744.

Karma Phuntsok Ling, c/o Manfred Bruckmann, Am Klapperberg 1, 6478 Nidda 28. Phone: (06402) 61 05.

Karma Sherab Ling, c/o Joseph Kerklau, Eineserstr 8, 4410 Warendorf 3. Phone: (0258) 8104.

Karma Sopa Ling, c/o Annegret Gulzon, Alte Meierei, Charlottental, 2301 Stoltenberg. Phone: (0430) 3316.

Karma Tengyal Ling, Oranienstr 183, 2 H H Aufgang B 4 Stock, 1000 Berlin 36. Phone: (030) 65 33 83.

Karma Tharpai Gyaltshen, c/o Erika Rosenfeld, Venloerstr 24, 5000 Koeln 1. Phone: (0221) 51 84 13.

Marpa Ling, Bissener Landstr 181, 2000 Hamburg 56. Phone: 81 44 70.

Meditationskreis, Frau A Petzel, Schoenaustr 58, 4600 Dortmund 50. Phone: (0231) 71.

Meditationskreis, c/o Rosemary Geisler, Salierstr 13. 8600 Bamberg. Phone: (0951) 545 54.

Meditationskreis, c/o Rose Enderlein, Mathildenstr 22, 2390 Flensburg.

Meditationskreis, c/o Dr E Thriemer, Wladstr 7C, 7000 Stuttgart – Degerloch.

Meditationskreis Hannover, c/o A M Buschbaum, Birkenkamp 6, 3002 Wedemark 14.

Muenchen Dharma Study Group, Aldringenstrasse 4, 8 Muenchen 19.

Mumon Kai Zendo, Fronauerstr 148, 1000 Berlin 28. Phone: (030) 401 30 69.

Odenwald Meditations Zentrum, Anke und Ueli Hirsch, Hoellgrund 18, 6930 Eberbach-Gaimuehle.

Pakshi Ling, Kircheweg 5, 6315 Muecke 1.

Phuntsok Matthatshang, Detmoldstr 6, 3000 Hannover 1. Phone: (0511) 81 71 09.

Tushita, c/o Wolfgang Juenemann, Wengerstr 8, 8961 Haldenwang.

Vajradhatu, Rigdenhaus Sherab Choedzen, Wilhelm Roserstr 29, 3550 Marburg. Phone: (06421) 61 220.

Wiesbaden Dharma Study Group, Wolfgang Burkhardj, Am Schalosspark 17, 6200 Wiesbaden-Biebrich.

Yeshe Choling, c/o Auwalstr. 22, 7800 Freiburg.

Zazen-Gruppe, Frau Christel van den Boom, Saalestr 4, 5300 Bonn-Ippendorf. Phone: (02221) 14 88 42.

Zazen Kreis, c/o Manfred Baaske, Am Ziegelberg 32, 6415 Petersberg b/Fulda. Phone (0661) 62530.

Zazen Kreis, c/o Gisela Vogt, Sixt-von-Arminstr 19, 6330 Wetzlar.

Zazen Kreis, Peter Vormschlag, Hulsbergstr 52, 4300 Essen. Phone (0201) 53 44 26.

Zazen Kreis, Werner Liebezeit, Aschen 96, 2840 Diepholz 2. Phone: (05441) 6541.

Zazen Kreis um Roshi Nagaya, Dr L Wolff-Rietzsch, Waldackerstr 19, 7000 Stuttgart. Phone: (0711) 87 52 64.

Zazen Kreis um Taisen, Deshimaru Roshi, Frau Collmann, Kalckreuthstr 3, 1000 Berlin 30. Phone: 213 65 55.

Zazen Kreis um Taisen, Deshimaru Roshi, Michael Andre, Beisserstr 23, 2000 Hamburg 63.

Zazen Kreis um Taisen, Deshimaru Roshi, H J Kremers, Sparenbergstr 33, 3450 Holzminden. Raum, Gottingden.

Zazen Kreis um Taisen, Deshimaru Roshi, Gunter Friedeberg, Scharnhorststr 9, 5000 Koeln 60.

Zazen Kreis um Taisen, Deshimaru Roshi, Thomas Quitschau, Celsiusweg 4, 2400 Lubeck.

Zazen Kreis um Taisen, Deshimaru Roshi, Ruth Ovie, Elsasserstr 45, 7000 Stuttgart 40.

Zazen Kreis um Taisen, Deshimaru Roshi, Ludger Tenbreul, Albendorfer Weg 2, 4404 Telgte.

Zen-Buddhistischer Freundeskreis Giessen Marburg Laut. Wilhemstr 14, 3550 Marburg.

Zen-Centre Hamburg e.V., Holthusenstr 15A, 2000 Hamburg 67.

Zen Kreis, Edith Schwarz, Karpfengasse 4, 7900 Ulm. Phone: (0731) 16 13408.

Zen Kreis Bremen, Wolf Dietrich Wolting, Fesenfeld 126, 2800 Bremen. Phone: (0421) 78659.

Zendo Frankfurt am Mein e.V., Robert Blum Str 5, 6000 Frankfurt/ M60. Phone: (0611) 44 45 14.

Zen-Dojo von Taisen, Deshimaru Roshi, Gerd Knauff, Alfred-Messel-Weg 12A, 6100 Darmstadt.
Zen-Dojo von Taisen, Deshimaru Roshi, Karin Furtwangler, Emil Riedelstr 6, 8000 Muenchen 22.
Zen Freundes Kreis um Roshi, Nagaya, Karin Stegmann, Rehmkoppel 17, 2000 Hamburg 65. Phone: 536 12 56.
Zentrum fur Tibetischen Buddhismas, Langwedelfeld 2, 2351 Langwedel. Phone: (04329) 337.

GERMAN DEMOCRATIC REPUBLIC

Buddhist Centre, Hale University, Hale, German Democratic Republic.

GHANA

Maha Bodhi Society of Ghana, PO Box 7148, Accra.

GREECE

Buddhist Society of Greece, Petaloudas 2, Ekali, Athens. Phone: 813 12 00.
Karma Drub Gyu Choker Ling, Pasteur 14, Ambelokipi, Athens. Phone: 642 75 81.
Peloponnesos Dharma Study Group, C/- Fritz Blauel, Agios Nikolaos Messinias.
Rigpa, 32B Academias Street, Athens 135. Phone: 362 57 07.

HOLLAND

Amsterdam Dharmadhatu, Ruisdaelkade 63, 1075 GG Amsterdam. Phone: 20 72 23 48.

Buddharama Temple, Loeffstr 26-28, 5142 ER Waalwijk. Phone: (04160) 342 51.
Buddhist Centre, Parallel Weg 14, 9717 KS Groningen.
Buddhist Institute, 499 Mient, The Hague.
Buddhist Union of Netherlands, Bornestr 61, 7556 BC Hengelo. Phone: (074) 91 75 73.
Dharmadatu, Valeriusstr 160, 1075 GG Amsterdam. Phone: (020) 72 23 48.
Dharmadpadma, Moerweg 428, 2531 BK, The Hague.
Groningen Dharma Study Group, Prof Rankestraat 30, Groningen.
Karma Chopel Ling, Henrik, Zabradreff 2119, Utrecht. Phone: (030) 61 80 45.
Karma Deleg Cho Phel Ling, Lama Gawang, Schoener 1423, 8243 TH Lelystad.
Karma Dhagpo Ling, Faustdreef 121, Utrecht.
Nyingma Centre Netherland, Postbus 1744, 1000 BS Amsterdam.
Rigpa, E Dissen, Kosmos, Prins Henrikkade 142, 1011 AT Amsterdam.
Sakya Thegchen Ling, V. Bleiswijkstraat 107, 2582 LB The Hague.
Upasika Vajrayogini, Ringidijk 90, Postgiro 16, 2586 Rotterdam.
Urienden V.H. Boeddhisme, Meidoornland 15, 1901 BT Castricum.
Utrecht Forming Dharma Study Group, Kroostweg 76, 3704 EQ Zeist.
Vrienden Van Het Boeddhisme, Eperweg 49-18 Nunspeet, 8072 DA Nunspeet.

HONG KONG

Buddhist Promoting Foundation, Room 65, New World Office Building, 20 Salisbury Road, Tsimshatsui, Kowloon.
Hong Kong Buddhist Association, 2nd Floor, 338 Lockhart Road.
Hong Kong KK Dharmachakra Centre, Flat A & B, 5th Floor, Maiden Court, 46 Cloud View Road. Phone: (5) 661123.

Hong Kong Buddhist Sangha Association, Winning Mansion, Block B 11, 12th Floor, Wong Nei Chong Road, Happy Valley.
Hong Kong & Macau Regional Centre, Lucky Mansion, Block G-H, 14th Floor, 18-24 Jordan Road, Kowloon.
Mui Fat Monastery, 22 Mile Stone, Castle Peak Road, Lamti, NT. Phone: (12) 81637.

INDIA

All India Buddhist Mission, 79/1C Biren Roy Road, West Calcutta 61.
Apo Rinpoche's Monastery, Chittiari PO Vashist, Manali, Dist. Kulu, HP.
Ashok Mission Vihara, PO Mehrauli, New Delhi 110030.
Bengal Buddhist Association, Naranda Square, 1 Buddhist Temple Street, Calcutta 12.
Bharateeya Baudha Mahasabba, Ambedkar Bhavan, Rani Jhansi Road, New Delhi 110055.
Bir Sakya Lama's Society, PO Bir, Dist Kangra, HP.
Bir Sakya Lama's School, Chowgan, PO Bir, Dist Mandi, HP.
Buddha Vihara, Anand Seva Sangh, Tagore Nagar, Vikhoroli, Bombay 400083.
Buddha Vihara, Plot 4, Unit 9, New Capital, Bhubaneshwar, Corissa.
Buddhist Association, Nubra, Dist Ladakh, Jammu & Kashmir.
Buddhist Association, Changthang, Nyoma, Ladakh, Jammu & Kashmir.
Buddhist Bharati, Silifuru, West Bengal.
Buddhist Centre, Nagasen Vana, Aurangabad, Maharashtra.
Buddhist Council of Bombay, C/12/2 New Quarters, Airport Colony, Hanuman Road, Vile Parle, Bombay 400 057.
Buddhist Education Society of India, Rissalder Park, Lucknow, UP.
Buddhist Mission, Port Blair, Andaman Islands.

Buddhist Sangha Nalanda, PO Nalanda, Mahavihara, Bihar.
Buddhist Society of India, Ambedkar Bhavan, Rani Jhansi Road, New Delhi 110055.
Buddhist Society of India, Ambedkar Bhaven, Gokuldaspasta Lane, Dadar, Bombay 400015.
Burmese Vihar, Bodh Gaya, Bihar.
Chorten Gompa, Deorali, Gangtok, Sikkim.
Council of Religious & Cultural Affairs of His Holiness the Dalai Lama, Gangchen Kyishong, Dharamsala, Dist. Kangra, HP.
Department of Ecclesiastical Affairs, Government of Sikkim, Gangtok, Sikkim.
Dhamma Kuti, 17/690 Buddha Vihara, Maya Link Road, Ajmer, Rajasthan.
Dharma Chakra Centre, International Kagyu HQ, PO Rumtek, via Ranipul, Sikkim.
Dharmankeer Buddhist Monastery, Noi Buddhist Temple Street, Calcutta 12.
Drikung Kagyu Centre for Buddhist Studies, Drikung Kagyu Monastery, PO Rewalsahar, Dist Mandi, HP.
District Buddhist Association, Kargil, Jammu & Kashmir.
Dre Gomang Buddhist Cultural Association, Lama Camp No 2, PO Tibetan Colony, Mundgod, Karnataka State 581411.
Drikung Kagyupa Monastery, Tibetan Settlement, Bylakuppe, Mysore, Karnataka State 571104.
Dudul Rabten Ling Gompa, Chandragiri, Orissa.
Dzogchen Orgyen Samten Choling, PO Odeyarpalya, Kollegal Taluk, Dist Mysore, Karnataka.
Friends of the Western Buddhist Order, Lipasaka Lokamitra, Pune.
Gaden Phegyeling Tibetan Mahayana Monastery, PO Bodh Gaya, Dist. Gaya, Bihar.
Ganden Shartse College, Lama Camp No 1, Tibetan Colony, Mundgod, North Kanara, Karnataka State 581411.

Gelugpa Cultural Society, PO Bylakuppe, Dist Mysore, Karnataka State.

Guru Sakya Monastery, Ghoom Monastery Road, PO Ghoom, Dist, Darjeeling, WE.

Himalayan Buddhist Association of India, Darjeeling, West Bengal.

Indian Buddhist Society, 207 Ghorpade Peth, Pune 2.

Indian Buddhist Society, Noor Lank Road, Byculla, Bombay.

International Meditation Centre, Bodh Gaya, Dist Gaya, Bihar.

Japanese Buddhist Temple, Bodh Gaya, Bihar State.

Japanese Temple, Saddhamma Pundarika Vihara, PO Rajgir, Bihar.

Khampager Monastery of the Tashi Jong Tibetan Community, Tashi Jong, HP.

Ladakh Buddhist Bihara, Bela Road, Delhi 110054.

Library of Tibetan Works & Archives, Dharamsala, Dist Kangra, HP.

Loseling Dratsang, Drepung Monastery, Tibetan Settlement, PO Mundgod, N Kanara, Karnataka State.

Mahabodhi Ashoka Mission, Dhamma Kuti, Buddha Vihara, Siddarth Marg, Mayo Link Road, Ajmer (Rajasthan).

Mahabodhi Society of India, Anand Vihara, Maha Bodhi Society, Dr Anandrao Nair Road, Bombay 8.

Mahabodhi Society of India, Mandir Marg, New Delhi.

Mahabodhi Society of India, Bahujana Vihara, Buddhist Temple Street, Parel, Bombay 12.

Mahabodhi Society of India, Chetiyagiri Vihara, Sanchi, Bhopal.

Mahabodhi Society of India, Dharmapala Road, Sarnath, UP.

Mahabodhi Society of India, 14 1st Main Road, Gandhingar, Bangalore 9.

Mahabodhi Society of India, Maragarah, UP.

Mahabodhi Society of India, 4a Bankim Chatterjee Street, Calcutta 12.

Mahabodhi Society of India, Kenneth Lane, Egmore, Madras, Tamil Naden.

Mahabodhi Society of India, Bauddha Vihara, Risaldar Park, Lucknow, UP.

Mahabodhi Society of Sri Lanka, 7 Chelmsford Road, New Delhi 110055.

Mulagandhakuti Vihara, Mahabodhi Society, Holy Issipatana, Saranath, Varanasi, UP.

Nalanda Buddhist Foundation, 18 Andhiari Bagh, Gorakhpor 272001.

Ngor Ewam Sakya Centre, Chowgan, PO Bir, Dist Mandi, HP.

Ngorpa Monastery Centre, PO Manduwala, via Prem Nagar, Dehra Dun, UP.

Nihonzan Myohoji, Japanese Buddhist Temple, Worli Naka, Opp Podar Hospital, Bombay 400018.

Nihonzan Myohoji, C/- International Culture Centre, J 22 Hauz Khas Enclave, New Delhi 110016.

Nihonzan Myohoji, Japanese Buddhist Temple, 60 Lake Road, Calcutta.

Nyingma Monastery, Arlikumari, PO Bylakuppe, Dist Mysore, Karnataka 571104.

Orgyen Kunzang Chokor Ling, 54 Gandhi Road, Darjeeling, 734101 West Bengal.

Pemayangtsi Monastery, PO Pelling, W. Sikkim.

Phensang Monastery, Phensang North, Sikkim.

Phodong Monastery, PO Dikchu, Sikkim.

Ralong Monastery, West Sikkim.

Retreat Caves, Tso Padma, Rewalsahar, Dist Mandi, HP.

Sakya Buddhist Gompa, Village Rangri, PO Manali, Dist Kulu, HP.

Samdrup Thargey Ling Monastery, PO Sonada, Dist Darjeeling, West Bengal.

Samiti-Babasaheb Ambedkar Samarah, Ambedkar Town, Dharampeth, Nagpur.

Sa-Ngor Chotsok Monastery, PO Gangtok, Sikkim.

Sera Monastic College, Lama Camp, Tibetan Colony, PO Bylakuppe, Dist Mysore, Karnataka State.

South India Buddhist Association, 41 Paddy Field Road, Perambur, Madras 11, Tamil Nadu.

Tai Situ Rinpoche, Institute of Buddhist Studies, PO Bir, Dist Kangra 175032, HP.

Tripura Rajya Buddhist Association, Venuvan Vihara, Kunjaven Agatara, Tripura.

Tsangdopede Monastery, Durpindarra, Kalimpong, West Bengal.

Tsegen Chokorling Sakyapa Monastery, Dist Mysore, Bylakuppe 571104, Karnataka State.

Tsechen Do Ngag Cho Ling Sakya Monastery, Lama Camp No 2, PO Tibetan Colony, Mundgod, Dist UK 581411, Karnataka State.

Tsechen Samdrup Ling, Tibetan Gaba Welfare Society, PO Kamrao, Dist Sirmur, HP.

Tsechu Association, 6 Mahatab Chand Road, Darjeeling, West Bengal.

Venuvan Vihar, Kunjavna, Agartala, Tripura.

Vipassana, Elysium House, McLeod Ganj, Dharamsala, Kangra District, HP.

Vipassana Centre, Near Galataji, Jaipur.

Vipassana International Academy, Dhammagiri Igatpuri, Dist Nasik, Maharashtra.

Vipassana International Meditation Centre, Nagarjuna Sagar Road, Kusumnagar, Hyderabad.

Zangdopelri Monastery, Kalimpong, West Bengal.

INDONESIA

Buddha Gaya Monastery, 10-23A Kelenteng Street, Ibandung, Java.

Buddhist Temple, Jalan Lembang, Jakarta.

Gabugan Tridharma Indonesia, 64-G Lautze Street, Jahunta.

Indonesian Buddhist Association, Jalan Cilacap 6A, Jakarta.

Indonesian Buddhist Youths Association, Jakarta Tebet Barat Dalam V1/24, Jakarta.

Sangha Agung Indonesia, Lembah Cipandiva, PO Sindangalaya, Cipanas, Pacet Java, Barat.

Sangha Theravada Indonesia, Alamat – 51 Terusan, Lembang D-59, Jakarta.

Vihara Maha Dhamma Loka, Jalan Dr Wahidin 12, Semarang.

World Fellowship of Buddhists, Indonesia Regional Centre, Gedung Lantze A, 3D Jakarta.

IRELAND *Republic of*

Dao Shonu, Dowth PO, Co Meath, Via Drogheda, Co Louth.

Dublin Forming Dharma Study Group, Avondale Ln, Albert Road, Sandy Cove, Dublin. Phone: 80 2954.

Dundee Buddhist Centre, 253 Hawkhill, Dundee OD1 2DN, Ireland

Rigpa, C/- M Leonard, 8 El Dorado, Milford Grange, Castleroy, Co Limerick.

ISRAEL

Dokyu Nakagawa, PO Box 436, Jerusalem. Phone: 02 271498.

ITALY

Amadeo & Sole Leris, Via de Merino Campagna, Rocca Di Papa, Roma.

Buddhismo Scientifico, Via Pindemonte 49 50124 Firenze.

Centro Karma Thegsum Tashi Ling, V Fontana Del Ferro 26/B, 37100 Verona.

Communita Dzogchen, Merigar 58031 Arcidosso (Grosseto).

Communita Dzogchen, V 11 Costed D'Agnano 34, 80078 Pozzuoli, Napoli.

Communita Dzogchen, Presso Barrie Simmons, Viale Di Villa Massimo 33, 00161 Roma.

Comitato Nazionale Okido Dojo, C/- G Magnani, P le Francia 9, 41012.

Dojo Zen, C/- F Guareschi, Via Berenini 11, 43036 Fidenza.

Dojo Zen, Via Nibbia 19, 28100 Novara.

Kagyu Mila Sherpa Dorje, Via Buniva 33, 10064 Torino.

Instituto Samantabhadra, Via Adolfo Rava 30, 00142 Roma. Phone: (06) 503 72 52.

Kagyu Mila Sherpa Dorje, Via Buniva 33, 10064 Pinerold, Torino.

Karma Thegsum Tashi Ling, C/- L Amadio, Via S. Giovanni in Valle 44, Verona.

Okido Dojo d'Italia, Via Nazionale 238/A, 61022 Cappone di Colbordolo.

Pal Karmai Cho Kyil Ling, Centro Studie Meditazione, Buddhista Mahayana Di Tradizione, Via Panama 1 00198 Roma.

Unione Buddhista Italiana, Via Pio Rolla 71, 1 0094 Giaveno, Torino. Phone: (011) 937 83 31.

Zen Rinzai Monastery, Podere Di Scaramuccia, Frazione Bagni 126, 05019 Orvieto Scalo.

JAPAN

Buddhist English Academy, 501 Grace Mansion, Shin Ogawamachi 3-17, Shinjuku, Tokyo 162.

Chuohji, Sapporo-Shi, Minami Rokujoh, Nishi 2, Hokkaido.

Dai Bosatsu San Zuigaku-In, Shimo Hatsukari, Hatsukari Machi, Otsuki-Shi, Yamanashi-Ken, 409-11.

Daimanji, Mukaiyama-4-4-1, Sendai 982. Phone: (0222) 66 6096.

Eastern Buddhist Society, Otani University, Koyama Kita-Ku, Kyoto 603. Phone: (075) 432 3134

Eihiji, Eiheiji-Cho, Yoshida-Gun, Fukui-Ken.

Hitzukenkai, Tokyo-Betsun, Minato-Ku, Nishi-Asabu 2-21-34, Tokyo.

Fukui-Ken, Yoshida-Gun, Elheiji, Sanzenkei.

Hitsuzenkai, Zen Calligraphy Society, 01-2-23-1 Shinagawa-Ku, Tokyo 140. Phone: (03) 775 6634.

Hokkenji, Moroika-Shi, Nasakawa-Cho 31-5, Iwate-Ken.

Hokkeshu Hommon-Ryu Shumiun, 1-26-4 Kitaohtsuka, Toshima-Ku, Tokyo 170.

Hokke-Shu Shinmon-Rye Shumucho Honryu-Ji, 330 Monya-Cho, Kamigyo-Ku, Kyoto-Shi, Kyoto-Fu 602.

Hommon Hokke-Shu-Shumuin, Myoren-Ji, 875 Myorenji-Maemachi Teranouchi-Dori-Ohmiya-Higashi-Hairu, Kamigyo-Ku, Kyoto-Shi, Kyoto-Fu 602.

Honganji International Centre, Nishi Honganji, Higashi Nakasuji, Rokujo Sagaru, Kyoto 600. Phone: (075) 371 5547.

Honmon-Butsuryu-Shu Shumuhoncho, Yusei-Ji, 110 Tokencho, Omae-Dori, Tchijo-Kudaru, Kamigyo-Ku, Kyoto-Shi, Kyoto-Fu 602.

Honzan Shungen Shu Honcho, 15 Nakamachi, Seigoin, Sakyo-Ku, Kyoto-Shi, Kyoto-Fu 606.

Hosshinji, Fushibara, Obama-Shi, Fukui-Ken 917. Phone: (07705) 205 25.

Hosso-Shu Shumusho, Kohfuku-Ji, 48 Norbori-Ohjicho, Nara-Shi, Naraken 630.

International Institute of Buddhist Studies, Dr Akira Tuyama, 5-3-23 Toranomon, Minato-Ku, Tokyo 105.

International Association of Shin Buddhist Studies, Ryukoku University, Omiya Gakusho, Nanajo Omiya, Shimogyo-Ku, Kyoto 600.

International Buddhist Institute, Zenyoju, Nishi-Sugamo 4-8-25, Toshima-Ku, Tokyo 170. Phone: (03) 947 6387.

International Institute for Buddhist Studies, 5-3-23 Toranomon, Minato-Ku, Tokyo 105.

International Zen Dojo, Seiteiji, Tsurushima 611, Uenohara-Cho, Yamanashi-Ken 40901.

Japanese Association of Indian & Buddhist Studies, C/- Dept of Indian Philosophy & Sanskrit Theology, Faculty of Letters, University of Tokyo, PO Hongo, Tokyo.

Japan Buddhist Federation, 1-5-5 Nishi-Askusa, Taitok, Tokyo 3.

Jodoshin-Shu Honganji-Ha Shumusho, Honganji-Monzenmachi, Horikawa-Dori, Hanaya-Machikudaru, Shimogyo-Ku, Kyoto-Shi, Kyoto-Fu 600.

Jodo Shu Seizan Fukakusa Ha Shumusho, 453 Sakurano Cho, Shinkyogoku, Chukyo-Ku, Kyoto-Shi, Kyoto-Fu 604.

Jodo Shu Seizan Zenrinji-Ha Shumucho, 48 Eikando-Oho, Sakyoku, Kyoto-Shi, Kyoto-Fu 606.

Jodo Shu Shumucho, 400 Eikando-Cho, Sakyo-Ku, Kyoto-Shi, Kyoto-Fu 606.

Ji-Shu Shumusho, 1-8-1 Nishitomi, Fujisawa-Shi, Kanagawa-Ken 251.

Kazuya Natsuo, 16 Nishin-Cho-Sasayama Hyogo.

Kegon Shu Shumusho, Todai-Ji, 406-1 Zohsi-Machi, Nara Shi, Nara-Ken 630.

Kenpon-Hokke-Shu Shumin, Myoman-Ji, 91 Hatadda-Cho, Iwakura Sakyo-Ku, Kyoto-Shi, Kyoto-Fu 606.

Kippohji, Yoshida-Gun, Kami-Shihi-Mura, Kippoh 35, Fukui-Ken.

Kodo Kyodan Honbu, Kodo-San Hon Butsuden, 38 Torigoe Kanagawa-Ku, Yokohama Shi, Kanagawa-Ken 221.

Koyasan Shingon Shu Shumusho, Koyasan, Koyamachi, Iyo Gun, Wakayama-Ken 648-02.

Maha Bodi Society, Seigoin Temple, 6-3 Kami Juku, Atami-Shi, Atami.

Maha Bodi Society, 8/1 Kanda, Iwatsuka-Cho Nakamuraku, Nagoya.

Maha Bodi Society, Hozenji Buddhist Temple, 24 Akabane-Dai, Kita-Ku, Tokyo.

Mirokusan, 926 Okawa Higashi Tzu Machi, Kamo Gun, Shizuuka 413-03. Phone: (0557) 29 0211.

Myokenshu Shumuhoncho, 718 Nomanaka, Nose Machi, Toyono-Gur, Osaka-Fu 563-01.

Nimpo Okuda Roshi, Shomjoji, Matsuo 1, Hinocho, Gamo-Gun, Shinga-Ken 520-16.

Ohbaku Shu Shumuhonin, 34 Sanbanwari, Gokasho-Ugi-Shi, Kyoto-Fu 611.

Reiyukai Branch, Chugoku, 2e 3rd Floor, Uchida Building, 1316-257 Okinone Cho, Fukuyama City, Hiroshima 720.

Reiyukai Branch, Chuuba, 3-15-5 Ayuchi Douri Shouwa Ku, Nagoya City, Aichi 466. Phone: (052) 733 3803.

Reiyukai Branch, Fukui, 1007 Narima I Chome, Fukui City, Fukui 910. Phone: (0776) 27 2610.

Reiyukai Branch, Hokkaido, 6th Floor, Dai 5 Fujii Building, 2 Chome Minami, Ichijyou, Chuou-Ku, Sapporo City, Hokkaido 060.

Reiyukai Branch, Kinki, 5th Floor, Toho Building, 45 Manya Nishino-Cho, Minami-ku, Osaka City, Osaka 542.

Reiyukai Branch, Kyuushuu, 1-11 Yamato-Chu, Kasuga City, Fukuoka 816. Phone: (092) 573 5031.

Reiyukai Branch, Miyazakori, 4th Floor, Uda Dai 5 Building, 1-24-1 Ohashi, Miyazaki City, Myazaki 880.

Reiyukai Branch, Wigata, Toukanbil Mansion 102, 1-2-6 Bandai, Niigata City, Niigata 950.

Reijukai Branch, Shikoku, Tamura-Cho Aza Nishiuchi, Takamatsu City, Kanagawa 761.

Reijukai Branch, Tohoku, 4th Floor, Royal Building, 5-1 Odawara Kongouin Cho, Sendai City, Miyagi 983.

Rinzai Shu Eigen-Ji-Ha Shumuhowsho, 41 Aza Takaino Eigen-Ji-Cho, Kanzaki-Gun, Shiga-Ken 527-02.

Rinzai Shu Enkakuji-Ha Shumuhonsho, Enkakauji-Nai, 409 Yamanonchi, Kamakura-Shi, Kanagawa-Ken 247.

Rinzai Shu Kencho-Ji-Ha Shumuhonin, 8 Yamanouchi Kamakura Shi, Janagawa-Ken 247.

Rinzai Shu Kennin-Ji-Ha Shumuhonin, 584 Komatsu-Cho, Shijo-Kudaru-4-Chome, Yamatooji-Dori, Higashiyama Ku, Kyoto-Shi, Kyoto-Fu 605.

Rinzai Shu Myoshinji-ha Shumuhonsho, Hanazono-Myoshinji-Machi, Ukyo-Ku, Kyoto-Shi, Kyoto-Fu 616.

Rinzai Shu Nanzenjiha Shumuhonsho, Nanzenji-Fukuji-Machi, Sacho-Ku, Kyoto-Shi, Kyoto-Fu 606.

Rinzai Shu Sohkoku-Ji Shumuhonsho, 701 Sohkoku-Ji-Monzenmachi, Imadegawa-Dori-Karagasuma-Higashi-Hairi, Kamigyo-Ku, Kyoto-Shi, Kyoto-Fu 602.

Rinzai Shu Tenryu-Ji-Ha Shumuhonin, 68 Susukino Babacho, Saga Tenryu-Ji, Kyoto-Shi, Kyoto-Fu 616.

Ritsu-Shu Shumusho, Tohshoda-Ji 438 Gojo-Machi, Narashi, Nara-Ken 630.

Sambo Kyodam, C/- Miyazaki Kanun Roshi, Komachi 2-16-5, Kamakura 248. Phone: (0467) 232010.

Sanshoji, Shichijo-Machi 679, Nara 630. Phone: (0742) 44 3333

Seikannon Shu Sensoji, 2-3-1 Asakusa Taito-Ku, Tokyo 111.

Seizan Jodosha Shumusho, 26-1 Nishi Jonouchi, Awao, Nagaokakyo-Shi, Kyoto-Fu 617.

Shigisan-Shingon-Shu Chogosonshiji, 2280 Shigibatake, Hedguncho, Ikomagun, Naraken 636.

Shingon Shu Shingi Shumusho, Negoroji, Iwade-Machi, Nagagun, Wakayama-Ken 64962.

Shingon Shu Sumadera-Ha Shumucho, 4-6-8 Sumadera-Cho Sumaku, Kobeshi, Hyogo-Ken 654.

Shingon Shu Sennyuji-Ha Shumusho, 27 Sennyuji-Sannaicho, Higashiyama-Ku, Kyoto-Shi, Kyoto-Fu 605.

Shingon Shu Toji-Ha Shumusho, 4 Katsuno-Machi, Nishikoguku, Ukyo-Ku, Kyoto-Shi, Kyoto-Fu 615.

Shingon Shu Yamashina-Ha Shumusho, 27-6 Ninnoudou-Cho, Kanshuji, Yamashina-Ku, Kyoto-Shi, Kyoto-Fu 607.

Shingon Shu Zentsuji-Ha Shumucho, 615 Zentsuji-Machi, Zentsuji-Shi, Kagawa-Ken 765.

Shingon Titsu-Shu Shumusho, Saidi-Ji, 1-1-5, Saidi-Ji-Shiba Cho, Narashi, Naraken 631.

Shingon Shu Buzan-Ha Shumusho, 5-40-8 Otsuka Bunkyo-Ku, Tokyo 112.

Shingon Shu Chizan-Ha Shumucho, 964 Shichijo-Higashiwaramachi, Higashiyama-Ku, Kyoto-Shi, Kyoto-Fu 605.

Shingon Shu Daikakuji-Ha Shumucho, 4 Osawa-Machi, Saga, Ukyo-Ku, Kyoto-Shi, Kyoto-Fu 616.

Shingon Shu Inunakiha Shumusho, 8 Okhai Izumisano-Shi, Osaka-Fu 59004.

Shingon Shu Kokubunji-Ha Shumucho, 1-6-18 Kikubunji, Ohyodo-Ku, Osaka-Shi, Osaka-Fu 531.

Shingon Shu Nakayamadera-Ha Shumucho, 2-11-1 Nakayamadera, Takarazuka-Shi, Osaka-Fu 665.

Shingon Shu Omuro-Ha Shumusho, 33 Omuro-Ohuchi, Ukyo-Ku, Kyoto-Shi, Kyoto-Fu 616.

Shin Shu Joshoji-Ha Shumusho, 3-2-38 Honcho, Sabae-Shi, Fukui-Ken 916.

Shin Shu Bukkoji-Ha Shumusho, 397 Shinkai-Chot, Takakura-Dori, Bukkoji-Kudaru, Shimogyo-Ku, Kyoto-Shi, Kyoto-Fu 600.

Shin Shu Izumoji-Ha Shumusho, 2-9 Shimizu-Kashira Cho, Takefu-Shi, Fukui-Kon 91501.
Shin Shu Kosho-Ha Shumusho, Horikawa Dori Shijicho Agaru, Shimogoyo-Ku, Kyoto-Shi, Kyoto-Fu 600.
Shin Shu Ohtani-Ha Shumusho, Joyo Cho Karasumadori, Shijicho Agaru, Shimogyo-Ku, Kyoto-Shi, Kyoto-Fu 600.
Shin Shu Sanmonto-Ha Shumusho, 2-3-7 Minori, Fukui-Shi, Fukui-Ken 910.
Shin Shu Takada-Ha Shumin, Senshuji-Nai, 2819 Shinda, Tsu-Shi, Mie-Ken 51401.
Shizuka, Reverend Haruki, Fuki-Chi In, Koya-San, Koya-Machi, Wakayama-Ken 64802.
Sohto Shu Shumusho, 2-5-2 Shiba, Minato-Ku, Tokyo 105.
Shoto Shu Shumusho, Horyaji 878, Horyu-Ji, Tgaruga-Machi, Tkoma-Gun, Naraken 63601.
Sohjiji, Thurumi-Ku, Thurumi-Cho, Kanagawa-Ken.
Soka Gakkai, 32 Shinono-Machi, Shinjuku-Ku, Tokyo.
Takeuchi, Reverend S, Kaihoji, Katsuura Onsen 642, Wakayama-Ken 64953. Phone: (07355) 20839
Tendaigimon Shu Shumuhonsho, 246 Enjoji-Cho, Ohtsu-Shi, Shiga-Ken 520.
Tendai-Shinzei Shu Shumusho, 3210 Sakamoto Honcho, Ohtsu-Shi, Shiga-Ken 5200-01.
Tendai Shumucho, 1771-1 Sakamoto Honcho, Ohtsu-Shi, Shiga-Ken 52001.
Tesshu Society, Chuo 1-17-3, Nakano-Ku, Tokyo 164. Phone: (03368) 0532
Toji Shingon Shu Shumucho, Kuko-Machi, Minami-Ku, Kyoto-Shi, Kyoto-Fu 601.
Vipassana, C/- Chris Weeden, 20-10 Higashi, Korie N-Cho Neyagawashi, Osaka 572.
Wa-Shu Shumusho, 18 Motomachi Tennoji-Ku, Osaka-Shi, Osaka-Fu 543.
Yosyoan, Ikeda-Shi, Yoshida Cho 179, Osaka.
Yuzu Nenbutsu-Shu Shumusho, Dainenbutsu-Ji-Nai, 1-7126 Hirano Uemachi, Hirano-Ku, Osaka-Shi, Osaka-Fu 547.
Zen Culture Institute, Hanazono University, 8-1 Subonoucho-Cho, Nishi-No-Kyo, Nakakyo-Ku, Kyoto 604.
Zuiohji, Niihama-Shi, Yamane-Cho 8-1, Ehime-Ken.

KOREA

Beobsang Nikaya, Pyeongchang-Dong, Seoul.
Beobwha Nikaya (Hanguk), Sanseondong, Seoul.
Beobwha Nikaya, Seongbokdong, Seoul.
Beop Youn Sa, 120-1 Sakandong, Jongro Ku, Seoul.
Bolib Nikaya, Soongindong, Seoul.
Bomoon Nikaya, Bomoondong, Seoul.
Central Mission of Ghondo-Gyo, 88 Kyongun Dong, Ghongno-Go, Seoul.
Cheontae Nikaya, Ganseogdonh, Incheon.
Chogye Nikaya, Geonjidong, Seoul.
Chogye Sa, Chongro-Ku, 110 Seoul.
Chongwha Nikaya, Jongro 2KA, Seoul.
Chungwa Nikaya, Nusanandong, Seoul.
Haeinsa Monastery, Gaya Mean, Hapchean, Kyong-Nam.
Hwaeom Nikaya, Ganseogdong, Incheon.
Ilyeob Nikaya, Seongbokdong, Seoul.
Institute for Overseas Mission, Won Kwang University, Iri City, Chola Puk Do.
International Meditation Centre, Song Kwang SA, Seung Ju Kun, Cholla Namdo 543-43.

Jeongsang Nikaya, Seoul.

Jineon Nikaya, Daebong Dong, Daeku.

Jingag Nikaya, Haweolgokdong, Seoul.

Korean Association of Buddhist Studies, Dongguk University, 26, 3-Ga Pil Dong, Chung-Gu, Seoul.

Korean Buddhism Chogye Order, 45 Kyonji-Dong, Chongno-Go, Seoul.

Korean Fellowship of Buddhists, Juntiah Building, 22 Hawolgok-Dong, Sungkuk-Ku, Seoul.

Maha Bodi Society, Kyongkuk Sa Temppe, 753 Jongreong 3, Dong Syong Booku, Seoul.

Taego Nikaya, Bongweondong, Seoul.

Weon Nikaya, Eeeli, Chunbok.

Weonhyo Nikaya, Changsindong, Seoul.

Won Buddhism, 344-2 Siu Yong Dong, Iry City, Cholla Pukdo.

World Fellowship of Buddhists, Box 591, Kwangmahoon, 15-4 Joung Dong Chungku, Seoul.

Yongwha Nikaya, Wansanadong, Jeonju.

LAOS

Wat That Luang, Vientiane.

WFB Regional Centre, Ministry of Religious Affairs, Vientiane.

LUXEMBOURG

Buddhist Group (European Union) C/- Roger Lentz, 49 Rue Marie Adelaide.

MALAYSIA

Beow Hiang Lim Buddhist Society, 503 Hill Railway Road, Penang.

Bodhi Panna Buddhist Association, 42 Jalan Zabedah, Batu Pahat, Johore.

Buddha Jayanthi Temple, 317A Jalan Pekililing, Kuala Lumpur.

Buddhist Association Baling, Kedah, Yeok Chee School, Baling, Kedah.

Buddhist Boys Brigade, 8 Jalan ACI, Muar, Johore.

Buddhist Choir & Meditation Centre, Chim Nam Garden, PO Box 1240, Kunching, Sarawak.

Buddhist Society, Maktab Perguruan Persekutuan, Bukit Glucor, Penang.

Buddhist Society, Maktab Perguruan Sri Pinang, Hamilton Road, Penang.

Buddhist Society, Maktab Perguruan Ilmukhas, Jalan Ceras, Kuala Lumpur.

Buddhist Society, University of Malaysia, Pentai, Petaling Jaya.

Buddhist Studies Class Sungai Siput, C/- Bro Chin Siew Wah, 41 Tingkat Ipoh Tiga, Ipoh.

Buddhist Vihara, 123 Jalan Berhala, Kuala Lumpur.

Buddhist Youth Circle Chetawan, Buddhist Temple, Jalan Pantai, Petaling Jaya, Kuala Lumpur.

Bukit Mertajam Buddhist Society, 1043 Jalan Berapit, Bukit Mertajam, PW.

Butterworth Buddhist Association, 6522 Jalan Kampong Paya, Butterworth, PW.

Centre Kedah Buddhist Association, C/- 68 Jalan Kuala Ketil, Sungei Petani, Kedah.

Centre of Humanistic Buddhism Malacca Branch, 177 Jalan Bandar Hilir, Melaka.

Centre of Humanistic Buddhism, 5 Pangkor Road, Penang.

Cheat Seong Hoon Buddhist Society, Youth Section, 388 Beauty Park, Ayer Itam, Penang.

Cheras Buddhist Chanting Group, 113-4, (3½ miles off Jalan Cheras) Kuala Lumpur.

Dalat Buddhist Association, PO Box 8, Dalat, Sawarak.

Dungun Buddhist Youth Circle, K-35 Jalan Lim Teck Wan, Kuala Dungun, Trengganu.

Grik Buddhist Association, 183 Batu Dua, N/V Grik, Perak.

Hoeh Beng Si Buddhist Mission, 18-A Jalan Raja Bot, Kuala Lumpur.

Hua Lian (National) Buddhist Study Group, 10 Racecourse, Taiping, Perek.

Ipoh Buddhist Fellowship, 132 Chamberlain Road, Ipoh.

Ipoh Buddhist Society, 47 Gopeng Road, Ipoh.

Ipoh Buddhist Youth Association, 14-A Pesara Satu, Ipoh Garden, Ipoh, Perak.

Jitra Buddhist Association, C/- Teh Kah Shim, 18 Jalan Ibrahim, Jitra, Kedah.

Kedah Buddhist Association, C/-Wat Nikodharam, Telok Wanjah, Alor Star.

Kelantan Buddhist Association, 3400 B-C Jalan Zainal Abindin, Kota Baru, Kelantan.

Kerpan Buddhist Chanting Group, Batu 14 Sampang Empat, Kerpan, Kedah.

Karma Kagyu Dharma Chakra Shedrub Dargya Ling, 64 Jin Beringin, Melodies Garden, Johor Baru.

Karma Kagyu Dharma Society, 22 Jalan-Jugra, Jalan Klang, Kuala Lumpur.

Karma Kagyu Society Ipoh, 16 Jalan Wu Lian Teh, Ipoh Garden (South), Ipoh, Perak.

Karma Tashi Choling Centre, 41 Tanah Rata, PO Box 7, Cameron Highlands.

Karma Tenjey Ling Centre, 1558 Rasa Road, Seromban.

Krian Vajrayana Buddhist Society, Lot 831, Jalan Siakap, Began Serai, Krian District, Perak.

Kuala Kangsar Vajrayana Buddhist Centre, 62 Taman Indah, Kuala Kangsak, Perak.

Kuching Buddhist Society, PO Box 1775, Kuching, Sarawak.

Kuching Tze Tin Buddhist Orthodox Association, 1st Floor, 85 Dan Hock Road, Kuching.

Mahindarama Buddhist Temple, 2 Kampar Road, Penang.

Malaysian Buddhist Association, Chemor Sub Branch, C29 Jalan Venus, Star Park, Ipoh.

Malaysian Buddhist Association, 3598 Jalan Ismail, Kotu Baru, Kelantan.

Malaysian Buddhist Association, 25 Temple Street, Malacca.

Malaysian Buddhist Association, Muar Sub Branch, 41-D Jalan Sulaiman, Muar.

Malaysian Buddhist Association, 159 Jalan Pasir Putih, Ipoh, Perak.

Malaysian Buddhist Association, Tangkak Branch, 53 Jalan Ong Siong, Tangkak, Johore.

Malaysian Buddhist Association Dharma Society, 70 Burmah Road, Penang.

Malaysian Buddhist Meditation Centre, 355 Jalan Mesjid, Negeri, Pulau, Penang.

Malaysian-Thai Buddhist Organization, Wat Chaiya Mangalaram, Burmah Lane, Penang.

Metta Lodge, 42 Jalan Sutera Sepuluh, Tamam Sentosa, Johor Bahru.

Muar Buddhist Society, 95 Jalan Haji Haib, Muar, Johore.

Nikkhodharma Buddhist Temple, Jin Telok Wanjah, Alor Star, Kedah.

Penang Buddhist Association, 168 Anson Road, Penang.

Pendang Buddhist Association, Youth Circle, Klinik Kerajan Pendang, Kedah.

Perlis Buddhist Society, 8 Seberang Kangar, Kangar, Perlis.

Persatun Budhis Universiti Sains, Universiti Sains Malaysia, Minden, Penang.

Persatuan Buddhist Nilayah Persekutuan, Wisma Buddhist, 3 1/4 Mile Klang Road, Kuala Lumpur.

Phor Cheow Huat Wan Buddhist Chanting Group, Jalan Chain Feri, Mk 15, Butterworth, PW.

Province Wellesley Vajrayana Buddhist Society, 486-489 Jalan Sungei Rambai, Bukit Merta Jam, WP.

Pure Life Society, Bstu G, Jalan Puchong, Petaling PO Kuala Lumpur.

Sakya Chospel Ling, C/- Mr Joseph Ling, Kwong Lee Bank BHD, 30 Main Bazaar, Kuching, Sarawak.

Sakya Gelek Rabten Ling, Bukit Mertajam, PW Penang.

Sakyu Kunga Choling, 14 Jalan Telok Panglima, Garang BT 23/4, Jalang Kelang, Kuala Lumpur.

Sakya Kunga Delek Ling, 44 Jalan Potter, Ipoh Garden, Ipoh.

Sambodi Buddhist Society, 39 Lanan Sungei Abong, Johore.

Sabdakan Buddhist Association, PO Box 1046, Sandakan, Sabah.

Sarawak Buddhist Association, 12 Ellis Road, Kuching, Sarawak.

Selangor Buddhist Association, C/- Buddha Jaynthi Temple, Jalan Pekeliling, Kuala Lumpur.

Sibu Buddhist Association, PO Box 369, Sibu, Sarawak.

Sitiawan Buddhist Association Youth Circle, 4 NG Kuok Garden, Jalan Lumut, Sitiawan, Perek.

Sunday Free School, Triple Wisdom Hall, 5 Pangkor Road, Penang.

Taiping Buddhist Society, 18 Upper Museum Road, Taiping, Perak.

Taiping English Dharma Youth Movement, Wat Bodhiyaram, 19A Creagh Road, Assam Kumbang, Taiping, Perak.

Taiping Lotus Dhamma Missionary Society, 491 Chong Sun Road, Pokok Assam, Taiping, Perak.

Taiping Lotus K.K. Dharma Society, 25C Jalan Patant, Kuala Lumpur.

Taiping Lotus K.K. Dharma Society, 491 Pokak Asam New Village, Taiping, Perak.

Taiping Vajrayana Buddhist Centre, 6-7 Loreng 4, Taman Assamara, Jalan Ayer Kuning, Taiping, Perak.

Tham Wah Wan temple, 196 3½ miles Klang Road, Kuala Lumpur.

Trengganu Buddhist Association, 80-81 Jalan Syed Zain, Kuala Trengganu, Trengganu.

Tze Yin Buddhist Society Kupang, 99 Jalan Gedek, Kupang, Baling, Kedah.

Vajrayana Buddhist Temple, 33 Pisang Road, Kuching.

Wat Bodhi Yaram, 19A Creagh Road, Assam Kumbangm, Taiping, Perak.

Wat Chaiya Mangalaram, Burmah Lane, Penang.

World Fellowship of Buddhists, Penang Regional Centre, 46 Dato Kraneat Road, PO Box 113, Penang.

WFB Selangor Regional Centre, Buddhist Temple, 123 Jalan Berhala, off Brickfields, Kuala Lumpur.

Young Buddhist Association of Kulim, 297-1 Jalan Tunku Ibrahim, Kulin, Kedah.

Young Buddhist Cultural Service, 38 Dickens Street, Penang.

MEXICO

Buddhist Promoting Foundation, c/o Mitutoyo Mexicana SA de CU, Walter C Buchanan 236-A, Fracc San Andres Atoto, Naucalpan, Edo de Mexico.

MONGOLIA

Erdenezhu Monastery, Ulanbator.

The Centre of Mongolian Buddhists, Gangdan Tekchingling Monastery, Ulan-Bator.

Enlightened Experience Celebration 2

Seven months of teachings, retreats and initiations in India and Nepal

From November 10th 1985 until June 26th 1986 a series of teachings, initiations and retreats covering the entire path of sutra and tantra will be offered by the Foundation for the Preservation of the Mahayana Tradition in Kathmandu, Bodh Gaya and Dharamsala.

And in December, in Bodh Gaya, *His Holiness the Dalai Lama* will give, for the first time, the initiation into both the generation and completion stage' practices of *Kalachakra*. The EEC2 programme has been structured to allow participants to attend this initiation.

Kathmandu, Nepal: Nov 10-Dec 14

The dharma celebration will commence at **Kopan Monastery,** overlooking the Kathmandu valley, with the **Eighteenth Kopan Meditation Course. Lama Zopa Rinpoche** and others will give teachings and meditations on basic Buddhism.

During the same period, **Lama Zopa** will complete the series of **Rinjung Gyatsa** initiations, which he started at the first Enlightened Experience Celebration in 1982.

Bodh Gaya, India: Dec 18-Feb 5

The **Kalachakra** initiation will start on December 18th. At its completion on December 27th, Gomo Tulku will teach for a month on **Maitri Gyatsa.** Starting January 28th, **His Holiness Sakya Trinzin** will teach for eight days on the **Thirteen Golden Dharmas.**

Simultaneously, throughout the month of January, **Tsenshab Kirti** will teach on alternate days on **Uttaratantra.**

Dharamsala, India: Feb 24-June 26

His Holiness the Dalai Lama has accepted our invitation to teach to Westerners in his temple, and has chosen the subject, **The Five Stages of Tantra,** which he will teach for seven days.

The last part of the celebration will commence on March 7th, with **Zimey Rinpoche** giving initiations into the practices of **Heruka, Heruka Body Mandala** and **Vajra Yogini,** and teachings on **Lama Chöpa** and **Heruka Body Mandala.**

Finally, a **retreat on Heruka Body Mandala** will start on April 11th and finish on June 26th.

For information about all aspects of the EEC2, write to the organizer, **Piero Cerri, Tushita Meditation Centre, 5/5 Shantiniketan, New Delhi 110021, India. Telephone 67 54 68.**

NEPAL

Anandakuti Vihara, Swayambhu Hill, Kathmandu.

Ananda Vihara, Palpa Tansen.

Buddhasasana Seua Samiti, Gana Maha Vihara, PO Box 993, Kathmandu.

Buddha Vihara, Dharan.

Buddha Vihara, Lumbibi.

Buddha Vihara, Pokhara.

Chandra Kirti Vihara, Banepa.

Dharma Swami Buddha Vihara, PO Lumbini, Dist Rupandehi, Lumbini Zone, 4504.

Dharmakirti Vihara, Naghal Tole, Kathmandu.

The Dharmodaya Sabha, Nepal Regional Centre of WFB, Ananda Kuti Vihara, Swayambhu, Kathmandu.

Dynakuti Vihara, Banepa.

Gana Maha Vihara, Ganabahal, PO Box 993, Kathmandu.

Holandi Buddha Vihara, Palpa Tansen.

Ka-Nying Shedrup Ling Gompa, Boudha Nath, PO Box 1200, Kathmandu.

Karma Sri Nalanda Institute, Buddhist Studies, PO Box 1094, Kathmandu.

Mahachaitya Vihara, Palpa, Tansen.

Mani Harsh Jyoti, Jyoti Bhavan, Kanti Path, Kathmandu.

Muni Vihara, Bhaktapur.

Nagara Kirti Mandap Vihara, Kirtipur, Kathmandu.

Nagri Gompa Retreat, Boudhanath, PO Box 1200, Kathmandu.

Nyingmapa Buddhist Monastery, Bauddha, Kathmandu.

Padmachaitya Vihara, Butwal.

Sakya Gompa, PO Box 1496, Bouddnath, Kathmandu.

Samaskrit Vihara, Bhaktapur.

Shechen Tennyi Dargye Ling, PO Box 136, Buddha Nath, Kathmandu.

Shakyamuni Vihara, Bhojpur.

Shiree Karma Raj Mahavihar, Swayambunath, PO Box 1094, Kathmandu.

Siddhi Vihara, Chainpok.

Srigha Vihara, Naghal Tole, Kathmandu.

Sudarshan Vihara, Banepa.

Sugatapur Vihara, Trisuli.

Yanglesho Gompa Retreat, Parping.

NEW ZEALAND

Buddhist Society, 4 Ripin Crescent, Meadowbank, Auckland 5.

Friends of the Western Buddhist Order, 5 Cluny Avenue, Kilburn, Wellington.

Friends of the Western Buddhist Order, PO Box 22-657, Christchurch.

Fullerton, Richard, Brighams Creek, RD2, Kumeu.

Golden Light Co-operative, PO Box 68-453, Newton, Auckland.

Karma Rime Thiksum Choling, Boddhisattva Road, RD1 Kaukapakapa.

New Zealand Theravada Buddhist Association, PO Box 1811, Auckland.

New Zealand Theravada Buddhist Association, PO Box 1167, Wellington.

Shere Group, PO Box 902, Tauranga.

Sri Lankan Buddhist Society, 28 Moffitt Street, Wellington 2.

Suvarnadhatu, PO Box 68453, Newton. Auckland.

Upasaka Indrajala, PO Box 22-657, Christchurch.

Vietnamese Buddhist Association, 6 Borlasie Street, Wellington 2.

The Wellington Buddhist Association, 77 Webb Street, Wellington.

The Wellington Buddhist Centre, PO Box 12311, Wellington North. **Zen Centre Auckland,** 2 Rautangi Road, Mt Eden, Auckland.

NORWAY

Buddhist Forbundet, PO Box 3706, Gimlevejen, Oslo 1.
Committee of Vipassana Meditation, C/- Ingeborg Haabeth, Uransem Borgyn 11C, Oslo 3.
Karma Tashi Ling, C/- Liv Henriksen, Aushallet 2E, N4000 Stavangar. Phone: (045) 89852.
Karmi Tashi Ling, Meklenborgveien, Oslo 12.
Knus Brennhoud, Strandveien 16, 1392 Vettre.
Vipassana, Kare A Lie, Semsun 53, 3140 Borgheim.

PAKISTAN

All Pakistan Buddhist Association, Golden Dragon Restaurant, Round Market, Islamabad.

PHILLIPINES

Chi Wee Temple, La Torre Street, Nr Narra Street, Tondo, Manila.
Karmapa Mahayana Dharma Centre, Room 907, Std Cristo Building, 497 Jamboneros Street, Manila.
Phillipines Buddhist Institute of Vajrayana Order, 1253 G Araweta Street, Tondo, Manila.
Po Chong Temple, Manila.
Po Chong Temple, 35 Benitez Street, Cabau QC.
Seng Guang Temple, 1176 Nara Street, Manila.

World Fellowship of Buddhists, Phillipines Regional Centre, 1176 Nara Street, Manila.

POLAND

Ehi Passiko, Gwardij Ludowej 12/23, PL 26-600 Radom.
Karma Dargye Ling, AL Zjednocrenia 11 m 43, 01829 Warsaw.
Karma Gyurmed Ling, C/- M. Kowalcsyk, UL Mazurska 42/7, 70424 Szezecon.
Karma Lodro Gyamtso Ling, C/- W. Czapnick, VL Radsikowskiego 152. 31342 Krakow.
Krakow Zen Centre, UL Lublanska 14 m 15, 31410 Krakow.
Lodz Zen Centre, C/- T Jagietto, Narutowicza 41/29, 90125 Lodz.
Myszknow Zen Group, UL Kozieglowska 64, 42300 Myszkow.
Torun Zen Group, UL Swierczewskiego 96/11, 86300 Grudiadz.
Wladyslaw Czapnik, VL Radsikowskiego 152, 31342 Krakow.
Zen Group Kattowitz, Piastowska 1/10, 41005 Katowicz.
Zen Group Warschau, UL Obonza 11/24C, 00332 Warsaw.

PORTUGAL

Ogyen Kunzang Choling, 50 Rua Do Breiner, 4000 Porto. Phone: 38 42 23.
Ogyen Kunzang Choling, 117 Rua Do Salitre, 1200 Lisbon.

SINGAPORE

Anandametrayana Buddhist Circle, 83 Silat Road, Singapore 0316.
Bo Tien Temple, 407/A Woodlands Road, 18.5KM, Singapore 2573.

Buddhist Promoting Foundation, C/- Mitutoyo, Block 2, 6th Floor, Units 601/8 PSA Multi Storey Complex, Pasire Panjang Road, Singapore 0511.

Buddhist Union, 28-29 O Jalan Senyum, off Sims Avenue, Singapore 1441.

Chee Seng Temple, 40D Jalan Murai, off Lim Chu Kang Road, Singapore 2470.

Chee Tong Temple, 305 Bukit Timah Road, Singapore 0922.

Chu Sheng Temple, 45 Lorong Lentor, Singapore 2879.

Foo Tee Tay (Clan Temple) 52 Middle Road, Singapore 0718.

Hock Leng Keng Temple, 43B Kampong Eunos, off Changi Road, Singapore 1441.

Hok San Teng Temple Association, 425C Upp Changi Road, 14 KM, Singapore 1750.

Hok Tek Chi Temple, 63E Telok Ayer Street, Singapore 0106.

Ho Lim Keng Temple, 20 Outram Hill, Singapore 0316.

Hong Kong Temple, 36 Loreng Sulur, Singapore 1955.

Hong San Temple Association, 271H Lorong Tai Seng, Singapore 1953.

Hoon Sian Keng Temple, 112 Changi Road, Singapore 1441.

Infinite Light, Buddhist Branch Culture Centre, 265, 2nd Floor, Bukit Tima Shopping Centre, Singapore 2158.

Jayamangal Buddhist Temple, 496 Siglap Road, Singapore 1545.

Jurong Temple Society, 20A Tao Ching Road, Blk 103, Jurong Town, Singapore 2261.

Kai San Temple Association, 1300 Jalan Bukit Merah, Singapore 0316.

Karma Kagyu Buddhist Centre, 17 Jalan Lateh, Singapore 1335 Phone: 282 4343.

Khai Leong Temple Association, 32 Jalan Tua Kong, Singapore 1545.

Khoon Chee Vihara, 23 Lorong Myaan, off Changi Road 5½ miles, Singapore 1441 Phone: 448158.

Kim Chuan Whuap Temple, 390 South Bouna Vista, Singapore 0511.

Kuan Yin Tang, 9 Loreng 13, Geylang Road.

Kuan Welfare Society, 86 Lorong K, Telok Kurau, Singapore Phone: 403091

Lam Hai Pohtoh Sanliansia, 825B Chuan Hoe Avenue, Singapore 1954 Phone: 880419.

Mangala Vihara Buddhist Temple, 30 Jalan Eunos, Singapore 1411.

Nanyang Buddhist Culture Service, Block 333, 1-13 Kreta Ayer Road, Singapore. Phone: 223 7190.

Ngee Ann Polytechnic Buddhist Society, 535 Clementi Road, Singapore 2159.

Phor Tee Lan Liao Temple, 37 St Patrick's Road, Singapore 1452.

Poh Jay See Buddhists Association, 34 Miri Road, Singapore 0409.

Poh Leng Jie Kwan Yin Buddhist Association, 14-16 Sennet Terrace, Katong, Seaview Palace, Singapore 1646.

Sheng Hong Temple, 300 Padan Gardens, Singapore 2260.

Shi Yun Lau Her San Hee Wien Tan, Block B, 26 Pacific Mansion, River Valley Road. Singapore.

Singapore Buddha Sasana Society, Sakya Tenphel Ling, 9 Topaz Road, Singapore 1232.

Singapore Buddha Yana Organisation, 26 Jalan Rabu, Singapore 2057.

Singapore Buddhist Federation, 50 Lorong 34, Geylang, Singapore 1440.

Singapore Buddhist Lodge, 17 Kim Yam Road, Singapore 0923.

Singapore Buddhist Meditation Centre, Blk A, Apartment 101, 50 Amberville, Marine Parade Road, Singapore 1544.

Singapore Buddhist Mission, Rev Mahinda, 9 Jalon Korma, Thomson Road, Singapore. Phone: 253 6511.

Singapore Buddhist Mission, 5 Namly Close, Singapore 1026.

Singapore Buddhist Prayers Society, Blk B, 26 Pacific Mansion, River Valley Close, Singapore 1024.

Singapore Buddhist Sangha Organisation, Phor Kark See, Bright Hill Road, Singapore 2057.

Singapore Buddhist Youth Fellowship, Crawford PO Box 724, Singapore 9119.

Singapore Buddhist Youth Mission, 18 Vaughan Road, Singapore 1335.

Singapore Chinese Buddhist Association, 21 Kreta Ayer Road, Singapore 0208.

Singapore Han Clam Temple, 2 Derbyshire Road, Singapore 1130.

Singapore Kim San Tze Temple Association, 125 Jalan Ulu Si Glap, Singapore 1545.

Singapore Kuang Chee Tng Buddhist Association, 125 Moulmein Road, Singapore 1130.

Singapore Regional Centre of WFB, 71 B Jalan Kechil, 32 Coronation Road, Singapore 1026.

Soon San Teng Temple, Senang Crescent, Singapore 1441.

Sri Lanka Ranaya Buddhist Temple, 30C St Michael's Road, Singapore.

Susila Budhi Dharma (Subud), 11 Jalan Buloh Perindu, Singapore 1545.

Taipei Yeun Temple, 7 Jalan Kemanan, Singapore 1232. Phone: 256 4941.

Tat Kwan Buddhist Institution, 774 North Bridge Road, Singapore 0617.

Temple of Lian Hong Sze, 293 Telok Blangaha Road, Singapore 0409.
Thai Temple, 83 Silat Road, Singapore 0316.

Tiong Ghee Temple, 1085 Stirling Road, Singapore 0314.

Tri Sarana Buddhist Association, 90 Duku Road, Singapore 1542.

United Five Temples of Toa Payoh, 1772 Lorong 7, Tora Payoh, Singapore 1232.

Wai San Buddhist Society, 57 Lorong N, Telok N, Telok Kurau, Singapore 1542.

Wat Uttamayanium Thai Buddhist Temple, Choa Chu Kung Road, Singapore 2368.

World Buddhist Society, 40 Pender Road, Singapore 0409.

World Fellowship of Buddhists, Bee Low See Temple, 71B Jalan Jurong Kechil, Singapore 2159.

Young Buddhist Editorial Board, 31 Jalan Hari Raya, Singapore 2057.

Zen Group, 12 Preston Road, Singapore 0401.

SOUTH AFRICA

Durban Centre of Karma Kagyu Samye Dzong, 4 Haven Road, Westville 3630, Durban, Natal. Phone: (031) 85 6609.

Karma Kagyu Samye Dzong, Port Elizabeth Centre, 44 Kruger Street, Mt Pleasant, Port Elizabeth.

Karma Kagyu Samye Dzong, 38 Geneva Road, Blairgowrie, Randburg 2194, Johannesburg. Phone: (011) 787 4624.

Karma Kagyu Samye Dzong, 1 Lulworth Mansions, St Andrews Road, Rowderbosch 7700, Cape Town. Phone: (021) 66 3591.

K.K. Trust South Africa, 21 Olympic Road, Blairgowrie, Randburg 2194.

Karma Kagyu Samye Ling, PO Box 15, Niev Bethesda, Cape Town 6286. Phone: (04923) 63 1693.

Natal Buddhist Society, 7 Harley Street, Havenside, Chatsworth, Durban, Natal.

Progressive Buddhist Society, 85 Paddy Park Road, Malvern, Durban, Natal.

Tibetan Friendship Group, 'Watersedge', 8 Malton Road, Wynberg, Cape Town 7800.

SPAIN

Dechen Ling, Centro De Estudios Tibetanos Alcalde Sains de Baranda, 57-8°D, Madrid 9. Phone: (01) 409 22 88.

Dojo Zen, Ramos Carrion, 6-6° pta 2, Madrid 2.

Karma Lodro Gyamtso Ling, Diputacion, 323-3-2a, Barcelona 9. Phone: (03) 301 97 68.

Palma Zen Centre, c/o Joan Insa, Tte Lizasoin, 1-4-2, Palma de Mallorca. Phone: (071) 23 82 89.

Samye Dzong, c/o Alvaro Urquijo, Miraconcha, 4-1°B, San Sebastian. Phone: (043) 45 29 61.

Serchöling, Centro De Estudios Tibetanos, Menendez Pelayo, 9-11, 3°, 1a, Sabadell, Barcelona. Phone: (03) 711 36 45.

SWEDEN

Buddhasana Forlaget, Box 5158, 2-102 44 Stockholm.

Buddhismens Venners, Friends of Buddhism & Swedish Buddhist Information Soc, Ringvagen 10, Bi Tr (4th Fl), 116 60 Stockholm.

Changchup Choling, C/- J Fritz, Sturegatan 2A, 752 23 Uppsala.

Kagyu Centre, C/- Jan Barmark, Vastra Hamngatan 3, 411 17 Goteborg.

Karma Shedrup Dargye Ling, Hokarvagen 2, Hagersten, 12 658 Stockholm.

Lotus Buddhist Order, Box 28013, 200 28 Malmo.

Nexus, C/- Peter Sandblad, Drottningaton 102, 111 60 Stockholm.

Svenska Buddhistiska Samfudes, Gotenburg, Mangatan 6D, 441 00 Alingsas.

Upasaka Aryavamsa, Ellenholmsvagen 11, 352 43 Vaxjo.

SWITZERLAND

Buddhist Dharma Centre, Thubten Changchup Ling, C/- Via Ruvigliana 11, 6962 Viganello. Tessin.

Buddhist Group, 4 Place Pepinet, 1000 Lausanne.

Buddhist Library & Dharma Centre, Academy Lloyds, 20 Rue du Marche, 1204 Geneva.

Buddhistjsherp Tempol Shingyoji, 14 Chemin Palud, Pregny, 1292 Geneva. Phone: (022) 347 65 58.

Buddhistische Gesselschaft – Zurich, Leh Franenweg 15, Witkikon.

Bulsong Sa, Buddhayana Vihara, Ches M Defago, 8 Rue des Asters, 1200 Geneva.

Centre D'Etudes Tibetaines, 8400 Rikon/Winterthur.

Dhamma Gruppe, Postfach 1410, 3011 Bern.

Dharma Group, C/- Dr Mirco Fryba, Allmendstrasse, 3014 Bern.

Groupement Bouddhiste De Lausanne, PL/ Pepinet 4, 1003 Lausanne.

Kagyu Chenpen Kunkyab, 5 Rue de la Parairie, 1202 Geneva.

Karma Cho Phel Ling, Gerechtigkeitsgasse 9, 3011 Bern.

Karma Sopa Ling, A He Meieteo, 2371 Osterade. Phone: (043) 3 44 13.

Karma Tenphel Ling, Samye Dzong, Armistrasse 18, 8908 Hedingen. Phone: (01) 760 18 18.

Lausanne Forming Dharma Study Group, Rue de Liseron, 1006 Lausanne. Phone: (021) 26 18 24.

Lugano Dharma Study Group, Via Monte Boglia 3, 6900 Lugano. Phone: (091) 51 88 83.

Thekchen Choling, Wettsteinstr 7, PO Box 25, 8332 Russikon.

Tibetan Institute, 8486 Rikon.

Union Bouddhiste Suisse, Hofwiesen Str 330, 8050 Zurich.

Yiga Choezin, Hinter Zunen 8, 8702 Zollikon.

TAIWAN

Buddhist Association, Republic of China, 6 Shaohing N Street, Taipei.

Buddhist Promoting Foundation, C/- Jain Dah Trading Co Ltd, 497 Cheng Te Road, Taipei.

Chen Li Li, 12th Floor, Block D, Shie Lin Ming Building, 25 Ashin Yi Road, Taipei.

China Academy, Institute for the study of Buddhist culture, 9th Floor, Ta En Pagoda, Hwa Kang 113, Yang Ming, Shan.

China Buddhist Research, 3rd Floor, 69-1 Yenping North Road, Sec 3, Taipei. Phone: 594 7035.

Fukuanshang China Buddhist Research Institute, 12th Floor, 328 Sunkiang Road, Taipei.

Karma Tekshe Tsomo, Institute for Sino-Indian Buddhist Studies, 22 Lane 110, Sect 2, Yang Te Road, Shi Tin, Taipei.

Kong Ga Shing Sher, 16 Lane 378, Chung Ho Road, Chung Ho, Taipei.

Lay Buddhist Association, Republic of China, 62 Min-Shen W Road, Taipei.

Torch of Wisdom, 10 Lane 270, 1 Chien Kuo Road, Taipei.

Vajrayana Esoteric Society, 3rd Floor, 17 Alley 330, Tun Hua S Road, Taipei.

World Buddhism Centre, 12th Floor, 271 Hsinti Road, Taipei.

TANZANIA

Buddhist Association of Dar Es Salam, Box 6665, Dar Es Salam.

THAILAND

Ashok Buddhist Centre, 65/1 Soi Tiam Porn, Klong Khum, Bangkapi District, Bangkok 24.

Buddhist Association of Thailand, 4 Phra Athith Road, Bangkok.

Chaing Mai Buddhist Association Youth group, Chaing Mai.

Maha Chulalongkorn Buddhist University, Wat Maha Dat, Maharaj Road, Bangkok.

Maha Makut Buddhist University, Wat Bovoranives, 248 Phrasumeru Road, Bangkok.

Thai Chinese Buddhist Association, 215/1 Pluplar Chai Road, Bangkok.

Vivek Asom Vipassana Meditation Centre, Baunsuang Muang, Chouburi.

Wat Absorn Sawan Vara Viharan, 174 Therothai Road, Bangkok. Phone: 467 0982.

Wat Arun, Arun Amartn Road, Con The Chao Phya River, Bangkok. Phone: 465 1989.

Wat Asokaram, Ral Ban District, Sammutprakan.

Wat Ba Pong, Ubom Province, Acharnchas.

Wat Ban Na Hua Chang, Canton Village, Pannanikorn District, Sakolnakorn Province.

Wat Benjamopitr (Marble Temple), 69 Sri Ayutthaya Road, Bangkok. Phone: 281 2526.

Wat Bodharam, Nakorn Sawan, Chiengmal.

Wat Buggachanarm, Bang La Mung District, Cholburi Province.

Wat Chakarvat, 225 Chakravar Road, Bangkok. Phone: 222 4949.

Wat Doi Pung, Tambol Pung, Prow District, Chitengmal.

Wat Doi Thammachedi, Thatn Phanom Road, 25 Km SE of Sakolnakorn, Nome Kai Province.

Wat Indra Viharan, Visuthikasat Road, Bangkok. Phone: 281 7810.

Wat Kowchalak, Bang Pra, Siracha, Cholburi Province.

Wat Muang Mang, Chiengmal, Chiengmal Province.

Wat Nern Panow, Nongkai, Nongkai Province.

Wat Pa Bahn Tahg, 89 Phosri Road, Thambol Ran That, Munang District, Udorn Thani Province.

Wat Paknam, Phasicharden, Thonburi District, Thonburi Province.

Wat Phra Keo, Emerald Buddha Temple, Grand Palace, Bangkok.

Wat Phraluang, Don Muang Village, Praea.

Wat Pleng, Sol Yingamnuay Charansidwong, Bangkok No 1 District, Thonburi.

Wat Po, 2 Maharaj Road, Bangkok. Phone: 222 0933.

Wat Raha Borpit, Fuengnakorn Road, Bangkok. Phone: 222 3930.

Wat Rajaphatikaram, 147 Rajvithi Road, Bangkok. Phone: 241 0828.

Wat Ratchborana, Muang District, Thonburi.

Wat Somnavora Viharan, 646 Krungkasem, Bangkok. Phone: 281 1018.

Wat Sraket, 344 Chakrapadipong Road, Bangkok. Phone: 223 6460.

Wat Sun Moke, Chaiya, Surat Thani Province.

Wat Sukontawas, Prupel Canton, Na San District, Suratthani Province.

Wat Suthas, Teethong Road, Bangkok. Phone: 221 4026.

Wat Threpsirin, 1466 Krungkasem, Bangkok. Phone: 281 0383.

Wat Tow Kote, Nakorn Sri Thammarat, Nacanton, Muang District, Nakorn Sri Thammarat Province.

Wat Trimitr, Golden Buddha Temple, Trimitr Road, Bangkok. Phone: 222 9015.

Wat Umong, Chiengmal, Chiengmal Province.

Wat Yannawa, New Road, Bangkok. Phone: 233 9927.

World Fellowship of Buddhists, 33 Sukhumvit Road, Bangkok.

Young Buddhist Association, 58/8 Pewkasem Road, Pasi Charoen District, Bangkok.

UK *England*

Acacia House Centre, Centre Avenue, The Vale, Acton Park, London W3.

ADMA, C/-Action Space, Drill Place, Chenier Street, London W1.

Bedfordshire Buddhist Society, 55 Larkway, Bedford. Phone: (0234) 66926.

Birmingham Place'Peace Centre, 18 Moor Street, Ringway, Birmingham B5 7UA.

Bristol Dharma Study Centre, C/- Jill Morley, 26 Archfield Road, Cotham, Bristol. Phone: (0272) 46266.

British Buddhist Association, 39 Elgin Mansions, Maida Vale, London W9.

Buddhist Promoting Foundation, C/- Mitutoyo UK Ltd, Unit 1, Kingsway, Walworth Industrial Estate, Andover, Hampshire SP10 5LQ.

Buddhist Vihara, 47 Carlysle Road, Edgebaston, Birmingham B16 9BH. Phone: (0214) 546591.

Cambridge University Buddhist Society, 122 Foster Road, Trumpington, Cambridge.

Cheong Gak Zen Centre, C/- N Battye, 4c Mecklenburgh Street, London WC1.

Chinese Yoga, 115 Sandy Lane, Cheam, Surrey.

Clacton Buddhist Society, 26 Beach Road, Clacton on Sea, Essex.

Cleveland Buddhist Group, 103 Overdale Road, Park End, Middlesborough, Cleveland.

Derby Buddhist Group, 9 Rothesay Close, Sinfin Moor, Derby.

Dhammaloka, 5F Manor Park Road, London NW10.

Hull University Buddhist Society, C/- Union House, Hull University, Hull, Humberside.

Institute of Tibetan Studies, (Prof D Snellgrove), Tibet House, 36 King Road, Tring, Hertfordshire.

Isolated Buddhist Group, Longfield, Cookshill Green, Chelmsford CM1 35J.

Kalpadruma, 43 Glenton Place, Streatham, London SW16. Phone: (01) 677 7381.

Kampo Gangra Shedrup Ling, Old Police Station, 80 Park Lane, Liverpool 17.

Karma Donga Kunchab Ling, 47 Carlyle Road, Edgbaston, Birmingham, West Midlands B16 9BH. Phone: (021) 454 2782.

Karma Naro, Middle Wenallt, Llanigon, Hay-on-Wye, via Hereford HR3 5OD. Phone: (049) 74377.

Karma Yong Dus Chopel Ling Buddhist Centre, 110 Lansdowne Road, Worcester WR3 8JL. Phone: (0905) 20104.

Karma Thubten Shedrup Ling, C/- J Berit & George, North Vale, Shire Lane, Chorley Wood, Hertfordshire HR3 6QD.

Khadiravini, 42 Hillhouse Road, Streatham, London SW16.

The Longchen Foundation. 30 Beinheim Crescent, South Croydon, Surrey.

Manchester Buddhist Group, 18 Burlington Road, Withington, Manchester M20 9QA. Phone: (061) 445 3805.

Manchester Buddhist Society, 3 Grosvenor Square, Sale, Cheshire M33 IRW. Phone: (061) 973 7588.

Meditation Meeting Place, 15 Hollins Walk Parkside, Reading, Berkshire. Phone: (0734) 586 897.

New World Centre, 'Pure Land', North Clifton, Nr Newark, Nottinghamshire.

Nihonzan Myohoji, Newland Farm House, Nr Willen Park, Milton Keynes, Buckinghamshire.

Northampton Buddhist Society, 93 Lutterworth Road, Northampton NN1 5JP.

Oxford Ashram, 99 Manbury Road, Oxford OX2 6JF.

Oxford University Buddhist Society, Linacre College, Oxford.

Pali Text Society, Balliol College, (Prof RF Gombrich), Oxford OX1 3BJ.

Plymouth & District Buddhist Group, 34 Torridge Road, Plymton, Devon PL7 3DQ.

Pure Land Buddhist Fellowship, Chittinghurst Farm, Todebrook, Wadhurst, Sussex TN5 6PQ.

Ratnadvipa, 34 Daventry Street, London NW1. Phone: (01) 258 3706.

Ratnadvipa, Upasaka Kamalashila, 22 Macroom Road, London W9.

Sang Ngak Cho Dzang, (Tibet Foundation & Institute of Tibetan Studies), South Hayes High Street, Ston-Easton, Nr Temple Cloud, Somerset BA3 4DJ.

Sarasviti, 12 Vivian Road, Bow, London E3.

Sarvasiddhi, 71 Kilburn Park Road, London NW6. Phone: (01) 328 1578.

Shropshire Buddhist Society, 10 Horsebridge, Minsterly, Shropshire.

Southend Buddhist Society, C/- D Keeling, 12 Marking Avenue, Westcliff-on-Sea, Essex.

The Springfield Trust, Fontmell Magna, Nr Shaftesbury, Dorset.

P Tanner, 43 Manor Road, Harbury, Leamington Spa, Warwickshire CV3 9HY.

Truro Buddhist Group, 21 Cardew Road, Truro, Cornwall.

University of Durham Buddhist Society, Department of Psychology, Science Laboratories, South Road, Durham DH1 3LE.

Vajracchedika, 95 Bishop's Way, London E2. Phone: (01) 980 4151.

Vajrakula, 41b All Saints Green, Norwich, Norfolk. Phone: (0603) 27034.

Vietnamese Buddhist Association, 12 Angus Road, Worthing, Sussex BN12 4BL.

West Surrey Buddhist Group, C/- Dr R Lever, Medical Centre, RACO Depot, Blackdown Barracks, Deepcut, Camberley, Surrey.

Zen Meeting Place, 40 Waylen Street, Reading, Berkshire, RG17UR.

UK Wales

Do-Ngak-Ling Rime Centre, (Buddhist Meditation & Study Centre), 36 Connaught Road, Roath, Cardiff.

Padma Ling, Uwyncelyn, Crosswell, Crymych, Dyfed SA 41 35B.

USA *Alaska*

Anchorage Dharma Study Group, 1507 Spar Road, Anchorage, Alaska 99501.

USA *Arizona*

Buddhist Church of Arizona, 4142 W Clarendon, Phoenix, Arizona 85019. Phone: (602) 278 0036.

Karma Thegsum Choling, 23024 North Evergreen Road, Phoenix, Arizona 85014. Phone: (602) 241 1883.

Phoenix Dharma Study Group, 3934 E. Picadilly 1, Phoenix, Arizona 85018. Phone: (602) 955 7455.

Phoenix Karma Triyana Dharmachakra, 3316 South Hazelton, Tempe, Arizona 95202. Phone: (602) 838 3864.

Tibetan Nyingma Institute, 11 West Jefferson, Phoenix, Arizona 85003.

Tuscon Dharmadhatu, 327 E. Helene Street, Tuscon, Arizona 85719. Phone: (602) 622 5560.

Tuscon Dharma Study Group, 2803 Via Rotonda, Tuscon, Arizona 85716. Phone: (602) 327 9250.

USA *California*

Adi Buddha Maddala, 2108 Shattuck, Apt 4, Berkeley, California 94704. (Yogi C.M. Chen).

All One Foundation, PO Box 31208, San Francisco, California 94131.

Bay Area Yeshe Nyingpo, C/- Tien Shou Hao, 2713 Grant Street, Berkeley, California 94703. Phone: (415) 848 1255.

Berkeley Buddhist Priory, 1358 Marin Avenue, Albany, California 94706.

Berkeley Buddhist Studies Institute, C/- Rev Kusada, 2717 Haste Street, Berkeley, California 94704.

Berkeley Buddhist Temple, 2121 Channing Way, Berkeley, California 94704.

Berkeley Zendo, 1670 Dwight Way, Berkeley, California 94703. Phone: (415) 845 2403.

Buddhist Association of America, 109 Waverly Place, San Francisco, California 94108.

Buddhist Association of San Francisco, 5230 Fulton, San Francisco, California 94121.

Buddhist Churches of America, 1710 Octavia Street, San Francisco, California 94109. Phone: (415) 776 5600.

Buddhist Church of Parlier, 360 New Mark Avenue, PO Box 547, Parlier, California.

Buddhist Church of San Francisco, 1881 Pine Street, San Francisco, California.

Berkeley Dharmadhatu, 2288 Fulton, Berkeley, California 94704. Phone: (415) 841 3243/3245.

Buddha's Universal Church, 720 Washington Street, San Francisco, California 94108.

Buddhist Fellowship of Sunnyvale, 12175 Hilltop Drive, Los Altos Hills, California 94022. Phone: (408) 948 8161.

Buddhist of Marin, 390 Miller Avenue, Mill Valley, California 94941.

Buddhist Temple of Alameda, 2325 Pacific Avenue, Almeda, California.

Chakpari Ling, PO Box 98, Forrest Ville, California 95436.

Chogyam Trungpa's Vajradhatu Centre, Padma Jong, Dos Rios, California 95439.

Cho-Ko Mountain Zendo, 108 South B Street, Mt Shasta, California 96067.

Chua Phap Van Vietnamese Theravada Temple, 850 W Phillips Boulevard, Pomona, California 91766. Phone: (714) 751 0361.

Darakshaw, 1761 N Harvard Boulevard, Los Angeles, California 90027.

Desert Vipassana, Dhamma Dena Retreat, Joshua Tree, California 92252.

Dhammadaya Buddhist Monastery, 115 S Commonwealth Avenue, Los Angeles, California 90004.

Dharmadana Jodo Shinshu Fellowship, C/- Rev K O'Neill, PO Box 796, Los Gatos, California 95030. Phone: (408) 356 6333.

Dharmadhatu Centre, 325E Canon Perdido, Santa Barbara, California 93102.

Dharmadhatu Centre, 57 Hartford Street, San Francisco, California.

Dharmadhatu Centre, 26120 W Freemont Road, Los Altos Hills, California 94022.

Dharmadhatu Los Angeles, 914 S New Hampshire, Los Angeles 90006, California.

Dharmadhatu Santa Barbara, 28½ Anacapa, Santa Barbara, California 93101.

Dharma Rev Suhi, 418 Ivy Street, Apt 2, San Francisco, California 94102.

Dharma Vijaya Buddhist Vihara, 1847 Crenshaw Boulevard, Los Angeles, California 90019. Phone: (213) 737 5094.

Drogon Sakya, 7284 Fountain Avenue, West Hollywood, California 90046.

Eel River Valley Dharma Study Group, PO Box 4682, Redway, California 95560. Phone: (707) 923 3891.

Enmyoji Buddhist Women's Association, 1200 Grastein Highway, Sebastopol, California 95472.

Enichizan Myohoji Temple, 7576 Etiwanda Avenue, Rancho Cucamonga, California 91739.

Ewan Choden Tibetan Buddhist Centre, 254 Cambridge Avenue, Kensington, California 94708.

Friends, 3624 Crosswell Avenue, Riverside, California 92504.

Garberville Dharma Study Group, 434 Maple Lane, Garberville, California 95440. Phone: (707) 923 3891.

Gardena Buddhist Church, 1517 West 166th Street, Los Angeles, California.

Genjo Ji Sonoma Mountain Sangha, Sonoma Mountain Road, Santa Rosa, California 95404.

Higashi Hongwanji Buddhist Temple, 503 E 3rd Street, Los Angeles, California 90033.

Institute of Asian Studies, 3493 21st Street, San Francisco, California. Phone: (415) 648 1489.

Institute of Buddhist Studies, 2717 Haste Street, Berkeley, California 95704.

Japan Bharat Sarvodaya Mitrata Sanghia, C/- Mr Takeo Koshikawa, 1645, Fairview Street, Berkeley, California 94704.

Jamez Bodhi Mandala, 2505 Cimarron Street, California 94102.

Jodo Shu Temple, 2003 West Jefferson Boulevard, Los Angeles, California 90018.

Kagyu Dharma, 6334 Telegraph Avenue, Oakland, California 94609.

Kagyu Dharma, 3918 24th Street, San Francisco, California 94110.

Kagyu Do-Nag Kunchab, 860 65th Avenue, Los Angeles, California 90042.

Kagyu Do-Nga Choling, 2711 Gilpin Way, Arcadia, California 91006.

Kagyu Droden Kunchab, 1892 Fell Street, San Francisco, California 94117. Phone: (415) 386 9656.

Kagyu Minjur Choling, Box 2, Ocean Parkway, Bolinas, California 94924.

Kagyu Penday Ling, C/- Kawa Family, PO Box 264, North Sea Juan, California.

Kagyu Tho Chen Jan Choling, 1114 Highway 101/S Downer, Encinitas, California 92024.

Kailas Shugendro Dharma Center, 2358 Pine Street, San Francisco, California 94150.

Karma Thegsum Choling, 23715 Camino Hermoso, Los Altos Hills, California 94022. Phone: (415) 941 7968.

Karma Thegsum Choling Center, 121 N Vulcan, Encinitas, San Diego, California 92024. Phone: (714) 753 9901.

Karma Thegsum Choling, 20 Anchorage Street, Marina Del Ray, California 90291.

Karma Thegsum Choling, 942½ S New Hampshire, Los Angeles, California 90069. Phone: (213) 387 9669.

Karma Thegsum Choling, Box 2211 Del Mar, California 92014. Phone: (714) 481 31977.

Karma Thegsum Choling Center, 135 Belmont Street, Santa Cruz, California 95060. Phone: (408) 423 1118.

Karma Thegsum Choling Center, PO Box 11 - 793A Palo Alto, California 94306. Phone: (415) 941 7968.

Karma Thegsum Choling Center, 2938 Cliff Drive, Santa Barbara, California 93109. Phone: (805) 682 1753.

Karma Thegsum Choling Centre, 447 Lincoln Boulevard, Santa Monica, California 90402. Phone: (203) 394 3906.

Karma Triyana Choling, 462 Rancho Sante Fe Road, Olivenhain, California 92024. Phone: (714) 753 4398.

Karma Triyana Choling, PO Box 701, Idylwild, California 92349.

Karma Triyana Choling, PO Box 285 Mountain Centre, California 92361. Phone: (714) 659 3835.

Karma Triyana Choling, 841 Mission Canyon Road, Santa Barbara, California 93103. Phone: (805) 969 4809.

Karma Triyana Choling, 9057 Harland Avenue, Los Angeles, California 90069. Phone: (213) 478 7741.

Karma Triyana Dharmachakra, 23715 Camino Hermosa, Los Altos Hills, California 94022. Phone: (415) 941 7968.

Karma Triyana Dharmachakra, 135 Belmont, Santa Cruz, California 95060. Phone: (408) 423 1118.

Kennyu Takashi Tsuji, 1710 Octavia Street, San Francisco, California 94109.

Korea SA, 239 S Wilton Place, Los Angeles, California 90004.

Koyasan Buddhist Temple, 342 E 1st Street, Los Angeles, California. Phone: (213) 624 1267.

Koyasan Buddhist Temple, 1306 W 253rd Street, Harbor City, California.

Lao Buddhist Sangha of USA, 938 N Hobart Boulevard, Los Angeles, California 90029. Phone: (213) 736 9058.

Los Angeles Buddhist Vihara & Buddhist Information Center, 1147 Beechwood Drive, Hollywood, California 90038. Phone: (213) 464 9698.

Los Angeles Centre, C/- L & K Clark, 2110 Glyndon Avenue, Venice, California 90291.

Los Angeles Dharmadhatu, 2853 W 7th Street, Los Angeles, California 90005. Phone: (213) 738 1909.

Los Angeles Hompa Hongwanji Buddhist Temple, 815 E 1st Street, Los Angeles, California 90012. Phone: (213) 680 9130.

Los Angeles Yeshe Nyingpo, C/- David Johnston, 11814 Stanwood Drive, Los Angeles, California 90066. Phone: (213) 398 9182.

Los Altos Zendo, 746 University Avenue, Los Altos, California 94022.

Los Gatos Zen Group, 16200 Matilija Drive, Los Gatos, California 95030.

Maitreya Centre, 307 Laguna, Santa Cruz, California 95060.

Marin Buddhist Church, C/- 14 Tamal Vista Boulevard, Corte Madera, California.

The Middle Path, 418 Pier Avenue, Hermosa Beach, California 90254.

Mongolian Buddhist Centre, C/- Mr Khendrup, 6322 Monte Cresta Avenue, Richmond, California 94806.

Monterey Peninsula Buddhist Church, 1155 Noche Buena Seaside, California 93955.

National Young Buddhists Association, 1710 Octavia, San Francisco, California.

Neo Dhamma, 2648 Graceland Avenue, San Carlos, California, USA 94708.

Ngor Ewan Choden, 254 Cambridge Avenue, Kensington, California 94708.

Nihonzan Myohoji, 82 Flora Street, San Francisco, California 94124.

Nihonzan Myohoji, 2674 S Vermont Avenue, Los Angeles, California 90007.

Ojai Foundation, PO Box 1620, Ojai, California 93023. Phone: (805) 646 8343.

Orange County Dharma Study Group, 3245 Indiana, Costa Mesa, California 92626. Phone: (714) 751 0361.

Orgyen Cho Dzong, 1909 San Antonio, Berkeley, California.

Orgyen Choling, 6448 Hillegrass Street, Oakland, California 94618.

Padma Ling Tibetan Meditation Centre, 2425 Hillside Way, Berkeley, California 94704.

Palo Alto Dharmadhatu, 156 University Avenue, Palo Alto, California 94301. Phone: (415) 325 6437.

Placer Buddhist Church, 3192 Boyington Road, Penryn, California 95663.

Redwood Valley Forming Dharma Study Group, 900 Lennix Drive, Redwood Valley, California 95470.

Rikzin K.D.K., 3476 21st Street, California 94110.

Rimay Chuday Tubten, 706 N Eucalyptus, Rialto, California 92376.

Rinzai-Ji, 2505 Cimarron Street, Los Angeles, California 90018.

Sambosa Buddhist Temple, 28110 Robinson Canyon Road, California 93923.

San Diego Forming Dharma Study group, 3957 B Miramar Street, La Jolla, California 92037. Phone: (714) 453 6109.

San Francisco Buddhist Church, 1881 Pine Street, San Francisco, California 94109. Phone: (415) 776 3158.

San Francisco Dharmadhatu, 1819 Jackson Street, San Francisco, California 94109. Phone: (415) 776 0502.

Santa Barbara Dharmadhatu, 28½ Anacapa, Santa Barbara, California 93101. Phone: (805) 966 5024.

Santa Barbara Dharma Study Group, 1129 'B' State, Suite 26, Santa Barbara, California. Phone: (805) 962 0978.

Santa Barbara Zendo, 333 E Anapamu, Santa Barbara, California 93101.

Santa Barbara Zen Priory, 509 Casitas Road, California 93103.

Santa Cruz Dharma Study Group, 915 River Street, Santa Cruz, California 95060.

Santa Cruz Zen Centre, 113-115 School Street, Santa Cruz, California 95060.

Sayagi U Ba Khin Memorial, C/- Michael Kosman, PO Box 304, Mendocino, California 95460. Phone: (415) 339 2462.

Seicho-No-Ie, 14527 S Vermont Gardens, California 90247.

Semshin Buddhist Church, 1337/6 W 36th Street, Los Angeles, California.

Shugen Church of Shugendo, 2362 Pine Street, San Francisco, California 94115.

Sino-American Buddhist Association, PO Box 217, Talmage, California 94581. Phone: (707) 642 0939/9946.

Society for the Advancement of Buddhist Understanding, 16925 East Gale Avenue, City of Industry, California 91745.

Somoma County Dharma Forming Study Group, 1531 Slater Street, Santa Rosa, California 95404. Phone: (707) 525 9498.

Southern Alameda County Buddhist Church, 32975 Alavarado, Niles Road, Union City, California.

Spring Mountain Sanga, 11525 Mid Mountain Road, Potter Valley, California 95469.

Sri Lanka America Buddha Dhamma Society, 2033 West Seventh Street, Suite 1, Los Angeles, California 90057.

Taegak SA, PO Box 57, Carmel Valley, California.

Tahl Mah Sah Zen Centre, 3505/3511 W Olympic Boulevard, Los Angeles, California 90019. Phone: (213) 732 9301.

Taungpulu Kabu-Aya Dhamma Centre, PO Box 31350, San Francisco, California 94131. Phone: (415) 826 2405.

Taungpulu Sayadaw Monastery, 18335 Big Basin Way, Boulder Creek, California 95006.

Theravada Buddhist Society of America, 68 Woodrow, Daly City, California 94014. Phone: (415) 994 8272.

Universal Buddhist Fellowship, PO Box 1079, Ojai, California 93023.

Vietnamese Buddhist Temple, 863-865 S Berendo Street, Los Angeles, California 90005. Phone: (213) 384 9638.

Vipassana Fellowship, 66 Melo Place, Berkeley, California 94702.

Vipassana West, PO Box 7234 (2145 McGee Avenue), Berkeley California 94703. Phone: (415) 549 1567 & 525 5091.

Wat Mongkalatanaram, 794 Grand Avenue, S South Francisco, California 94080. Phone: (415) 589 8120.

Wat Thai, 12909 Cantara Street, N Hollywood, California 91605. Phone: (213) 989 9679.

Yeshi Nyingpo, 1806 Tenth Avenue, Oakland, California 94606. Phone: (415) 261 0620.

Yeshi Nyingpo, 6938 Portola Drive, El Cerrito, California 94530.

Zen Centre, 300 Page Street, San Francisco, California 94102.

Zen Centre Green Gulch Farm, Star Route, Sausalito, California 94965.

Zen Centre of Long Beach, 1942 Magnolia Avenue, Long Beach, California 90806.

Zen Centre of Los Angeles, 927/905 S. Normandie Avenue, Los Angeles, California 90006. Phone: (213) 387 2351.

Zen Mission Society, Shasta Abbey, Route 1, Box 578 AI, California 96067.

USA Colorado

Denver Dharma Study Group, 3182 W 35th Avenue, Denver, Colorado 80211. Phone: (303) 477 0863.

Denver Zen Centre, 1233 Columbine, Denver, Colorado 80206.

Dorjee Khyung Dzong, PO Box 55, Farasita, Colorado 81037.

Insight Meditation Institute C/- Keith Meagher, 2324 Grape Street, Denver, Colorado 80207. Phone: (303) 321 3572.

La Jara Buddhist Church, La Jara, Colorado 81140.

Karma Dzong, 1345 Spruce Street, Boulder, Colorado 80302.

Karma Joman Lodni, 2755 7th Street, Boulder, Colorado 80302.

Maitri Psychological Service, 550 Mapleton Avenue, Boulder, Colorado 80302.

Marpa House, 891 12th Street, Boulder, Colorado 80302.

Naropa Institute, 1111 Pearl Street, Boulder, Colorado 80302.

Nyingma Institute, 1441 Broadway, Boulder, Colorado. Phone: (303) 443 5550.

Rocky Mountain Dharma centre, Red Feather Lakes, Colorado 80545.

Rocky Mountain Dharma Centre, Route 1, Livermore, Colorado 80536.

Tri-State Buddhist Church, 1947 Lawrence Street, Denver, Colorado 80202. Phone: (303) 623 1893.

Vietnamese Buddhist Pagoda, 369 S Pearl Street, Denver, Colorado 80209. Phone: (303) 722 7662.

Wat Buddha Wararam of Denver, 4801 Julian Street, Denver, Colorado 80221. Phone: (303) 433 1826.

Zen Centre of Denver, 1233 Columbine Street, Denver, Colorado 80206. Phone: (303) 333 4844.

USA *Connecticut*

New Haven Dharma Study Group, 194 Dwight Street, New Haven, Connecticut 06511. Phone: (203) 624 7446.
New Haven Forming Dharma Study Group, 1908 Chapel Street, New Haven, Connecticut 06515. Phone: (203) 389 1260.

USA *Florida*

Atlantic Beach Forming Dharma Study Group, 10 10th Street, Atlantic Beach, Florida 32233. Phone: (904) 249 8419.
Augusta Buddhist Group, C/- Bill Finney, 12 Tower Apartments, Carrollton, Georgia, Florida 30018.
Dharmadhatu Miami, 4555 SW 58th Avenue, Miami, Florida 33155. Phone: (305) 666 8836.
Insight Meditation Group, 2220 SW 34th Street, Apt 186, Gainesville, Florida 32605. Phone: (904) 375 4255.
Miami Dharmadhatu, 5793 Commerce Lane, Miami, Florida 33143. Phone: (305) 433 1233.
Tallahassee Dharma Study Group, 164-4 Crenshaw Drive, Tallahassee, Florida 32304. Phone: (901) 576 6940.
Vipassana South Meditation Center, 15330 South River Drive, Miami, Florida 33169. Phone: (305) 685 8816/8851.
Wat Mongkolrataram of Florida 5306 Palm River Road, Tampa, Florida 33619. Phone: (813) 621 1669.

USA *Georgia*

Atlanta Dharmadhatu, 3179 Peachtree Road NE, Atlanta, Georgia 30305. Phone: (404) 262 2527.
Wat Buddha Bucha, Doraville, Georgia.
Zen Group, C/- P de Sercey, Burwell Road, Carrollton, Georgia 30017. Phone: (404) 834 0571.

USA *Hawaii*

Dae Won Sa, Korean Buddhist Temple, 2559 Walomao Road, Honolulu, Hawaii. Phone: (808) 947 7117.
Diamond Sangha Koko-An Zendo, 2119 Kaloa Way, Honolulu, Hawaii 96822. Phone: (808) 946 0666.
Hongwanji Buddhist Mission of Hawaii, 1727 Pali Highway, Honolulu, Hawaii 96813. Phone: (808) 538 3805.
Jakkozan Honseiji, 44-668 Kaneohe Bay Drive, Kaneohe, Hawaii 96744.
Jodo Mission of Hawaii, 1429 Makiki Street, Honolulu, Hawaii 96822.
Kagyu Dhexhen Hermitage, C/- Jeff Munoz, Box 63, Makawao, Hawaii 96768.
Kahului Jodo Mission, PO Box 1482. Kahului, Hawaii 96732.
Karma Rimay Sal Ling, PO Box 571, Makawao, Mui, Hawaii 96786. Phone: (808) 572 1670.
K/Loloa Hongwanji Kyodan, PO Box 445, Koloa, Hawaii 96750.
Koloa Jodo Mission, PO Box 457, Koloa Kuai, Hawaii 96756.
Koon Yum Temple, 170 N Vineyard Boulevard, Honululu, Hawaii.
Lahaina Jodo Mission, 12 Ala Moana Street, Lahaina, Maui, Hawaii 96761.
Lihue Hongwanji Mission, PO Box 1148, Lihue, Kaui, Hawaii.
Masao Ichishma, Tenda Mission of Hawaii, 23 Jack Ln, Honolulu, Hawaii 96816.
Moilili Hongwanji Mission, 902 University Avenue, Honolulu, Hawaii 96814.

Nechung Drayang Ling, PO Box 281, Pahala, Hawaii 96777. Phone: (808) 928 8539.
Rimay O Sal Ling, C/- Ann Gronquist, Star Rt, 41 Hainku, Maui, Hawaii 96813.
Rimay Shedrup Ling Tubten, PO Box 701, Pahala, Hawaii 96777.
Shing Lung Gompa, PO Box 701, Pahala, Hawaii 96777.
Situ Rimay Choling, 2490 Tantalus Drive, Honolulu, Hawaii 96813.
Situ Rimay Choling Retreat, 53-086 Halai Street, Hauula, Hawaii 96717. Phone: (808) 293 8657.
Soto Mission of Hawaii, 1708 Nuanu Avenue, Honolulu, Hawaii 96817.
Wailuku Hongwanji Mission, 1828 Vineyard Street, Wailuku, Hawaii 96793.
Waimea Higashi Hongwanji, Waimea Kauau, Hawaii 96796.

USA *Idaho*

Idaho Dharmadhatu, Rt 1, Kimberley, Idaho 83341. Phone: (208) 734 7043.
Idaho Oregon Buddhist Church, PO Box 364 (286 SE 4th Sd), Ontario, Idaho 97914. Phone: (503) 899 8562.

USA *Illinois*

Bul Ta Sah Temple, 3437 N Daneman Avenue, Chicago, Illinois 60618.
Chicago Karma Thegsum Choling Centre, C/- Martinez, 6517 N Bosworth, Chicago, Illinois 60626. Phone: (312) 743 6247.
Chicago Zen Buddhist Church, 2230 N Halvstead Street, Chicago, Illinois 60640.
Chua Quang Minh Temple, 1702 N Rockwell Street, Chicago, Illinois 60647.
Daibeizan Myogyoji, 1 S 100 Route 59, West Chicago, Illinois 60185.
Dharmadhatu Chicago, 640 N State Street, Chicago 60610, Illinois. Phone: (312) 649 9892.
Dhammaram Temple, 1000 1004 N Hoyne Avenue, Chicago, Illinois 60622. Phone: (313) 486 9017.
Karma Triyana Choling, 7409 W 13th Street, Cicero, Illinois 60650. Phone: (312) 863 3429.
Maha Bodhi Society, 1151 W Leland Avenue, Chicago, Illinois 60640.
Midwest Buddhist Church, 435 W Menomonee Street, Chicago, Illinois 60614. Phone: (312) 943 7801.

USA *Indiana*

Bloomington Dharmadhatu, Route 12, Box 340A, Bloomington, Indiana 47401.
Chambaling Inc., Route 1, Box 9, Nashville, Indiana 47447.
The Tibet Society, Goodbody Hall 157, Indiani University, Bloomington, Indiana 47405. Phone: (812) 337 4339.

USA *Kentucky*

Lexington Dharma Study Group, 361 Transylvania Park, Lexington, Kentucky 40508. Phone: (606) 252 1116.
Lexington Zen Centre, 345 Jesselin Drive, Lexington, Kentucky 56403. Phone: (606) 277 2438.

USA *Louisiana*

Baton Rouge Dharma Study Group, 775 Nelson Drive, Baton Rouge, Louisiana 70808. Phone: (504) 766 1487.
New Orleans Dharma Study Group, Rt 3, Box 372, Cowinton, Louisiana 70433. Phone: (504) 1538.

USA *Maine*

Bangor Dharma Study Group, 240 W Broadway, Bangor, Maine 04401. Phone: (207) 942 9331.
Bath Zen Group, C/- Highsmith Hathaway, Cheqonski Foundation, Wiscasset, Maine 04579.
Dharma Study Group, C/- 8, Cobb Route 4, Box 34, Bangor, Maine 04401.

USA *Maryland*

Baltimore Dharma Study Group, 2408 N Charles St, Baltimore, Maryland 21218. Phone: (301) 323 7544.
Baltimore Zen Group, 1100 Bryn Mawr Road, Baltimore, Maryland 21210.
Burmese American Buddhist Association, 1708 Powder Mill Road, Silver Spring, Maryland 20903.
Dharmadhatu Centre, 4608 Doset Avenue, Chevy Chase, Maryland 20015.
Rock Creek Temple of America, 738 S 22 St Arlington, Maryland 22202. Phone: (703) 920 8978.
Wat Buddhamongroc. 705 Wayne Avenue, Silver Springs, Maryland 20910.

Wat Thati, 9033 Georgia Avenue, Silver Springs, Maryland 20910. Phone: (301) 585 5215.

USA *Massachusetts*

American Buddhist Shim Gum Do Association, 203 Chestnut Hill Avenue, Brighton, Massachusetts 02135. Phone: (617) 787 1506.
Boston Karma Thegsum Choling, C/- S Zimmerman, 45 Copeland Street, Watertown, Massachusetts 02172. Phone: (617) 926 4760.
Buddhayana Foundation, 15 Main Street, Marion, Massachusetts 02738.
Cambridge Buddhist Association, 75 Sparks Street, Cambridge, Massachusetts.
Cambridge Zen Centre, 263 N Harvard Street, Allston, Massachusetts 02134. Phone: (617) 254 0363.
Cape Ann Zen Centre, C/- Linda Parker, 2 Stage Fort, Gloucester, Massachusetts 01930. Phone: (617) 283 9308.
Dharmadhatu Centre, 169 B Upland Road, Cambridge, Massachusetts 02140.
Dharma Study Group, C/- A Stevens, 25 Main Street, Worthington, Massachusetts 01060. Phone: (413) 584 3956.
Kagyu Tinley Kunchab, 7 Athens Street, Cambridge, Massachusetts 02138. Phone: (617) 868 5248.
Kagyu Thinley Kunchab, Madeline Nold, 59 Highland Avenue, Winchester, Massachusetts 01890. Phone: (617) 729 8897.
Sakya Shei Drup Ling, C/- Johnston, 41a Harrison Street, Summerville, Massachusetts 02143.
Sayagi U Ba Khin Memorial, C/- Michael Stein, Roaring Brook Road, Conway, Massachusetts 01341. Phone: (413) 369 4090.
U Ba Khin Trust, Box 24, Shelbourne Falls, Massechusetts 01370.
Valley Zendo, Warner Hill Road, Charlemont, Massechusetts 01339.

Vipassana Fellowship of America, 41 Stearns Avenue, Medford, Massachusetts 02155.
Vipassana Fellowship of America, Chapelbrook, Ashfield Road, Williamsburg, Massachusetts 01906. Phone: (413) 628 3243.
Yeshe Nyingpo, 172 Naples Road, Brookling, Massachusetts 02146. Phone: (617) 277 2674.

USA *Michigan*

Ann Arbor Dharma Study Group, 510 8th Avenue, Ann Arbor, Michigan 48104. Phone: (313) 665 4481.
Battle Creek Dharma Study Group, 349 Main Street, Battle Creek, Michigan 49017. Phone: (616) 965 5217.
Chogyam Trungpa's Dharmadhatu Centre, 727 Madison Place, Ann Arbor, Michigan 48104.
Chua Linh-Son Buddhist Temple, 14271 Houston-Whittier Ave, Detroit, Michigan 48205. Phone: (313) 839 0730.
Dharmadatu Centre, 727 Madison Place, Ann Arbor, Michigan 48104.
Karma Triyana Choling, 734 Fountain Street, Ann Arbor, Michigan 48104. Phone: (313) 994 6657.
Karma Triyana Dharmachakra, 1219 Wright Street, Ann Arbor, Michigan 48105. Phone: (313) 769 2454.
So Getsu In, Box 39, Fremont, Michigan 49412.
Zen Buddhist Temple, 1214 Packard Avenue, Ann Arbor, Michigan 48104.

USA *Minnesota*

Minnesota Zen Meditation Centre, 3343E Calhoun Parkway, Minneapolis, Minnesota 55408.

Sakya Thupten Gargue Ling, 1615 Bruce Avenue, Roseville, Minnesota 55113.
Twin Cities Zendo, 136 Amherst Street, St Pauls, Minnesota 55105.

USA *Missouri*

Dharma Study Group, C/- D Katz, 6678 Washington Avenue, University City, Missouri 63130. Phone: (314) 862 4931.
Heartland Insight Meditation Network, 427 S Main, Carthage, Missouri 64836.
Kansas City Dharma Study Group, 3529 N Kenwood, Kansas City, Missouri 64116. Phone: (816) 452 0733.
Lawrence Chogye Zen Group, 413 Yorkshire Drive, Lawrence, Kansas, Missouri 66044. Phone: (913) 842 9093.
Zen Meditation Group, 6007 Pershing Apt 2E, St Louis, Missouri 63112. Phone: (314) 862 0178.

USA *North Carolina*

Durham Chapel Hill Dharma Study Group, 1200 Markham Avenue, Durham, North Carolina, 27701. Phone: (919) 286 1487.
Durham Dharma Study Group, 108 N Buchanan, Durham, North Carolina. Phone: (919) 489 0251.
Karma Thegsum Choling, Box 149, A8 Rt 1, Pittsbord, North Carolina 27312. Phone: (919) 967 9615.
Mountain Dharma Centre, Rt 1, Box 158A, Boone, North Carolina 28607.
North Carolina Karma Thegsum Choling, 707 E Franklin Street, Chapel Hill, North Carolina 27514.

USA *Nebraska*

Dharma Study Group, C/- Dave Schulze, Dept of Economics, University of Omaha, PO Box 688, Omaha, Nebraska 68131.
Omaha Zen Group, 1915 N 84th Street, Omaha, Nebraska 68114.

USA *New Hampshire*

Dharma Study Group, C/- J Korbel, Box 614, Durham, New Hampshire 03824.
Kagyu Osal Chudzong, RFD 84A, Connor Pond Road, Ctr Ossipie, New Hampshire 03814.

USA *New Jersey*

Buddhist Promotion Foundation, 18 Essex Road, Paramus, New Jersey 07652.
Institute for Studies of World Religion, C/- Dr C T Shen, 2150 Center Avenue, Fort Lee, New Jersey 07024.
Lamaist Buddhist Monastery of America, Box 306A Road 1, Washington, New Jersey 0782. Phone: (201) 689 6080.
Lamaist Buddhist Monastery of America, 281 Hamilton Street, New Brunswick, New Jersey 18910. Phone: (201) 249 2549.
Matawan Dharma Study Group, 53 Juniper Pl, Matawan, New Jersey 07747. Phone: (201) 583 4447.
Rashi Gempil Ling First Kalmuk Buddhist Temple, RD 3, Box 90, Howell, New Jersey 07731. Phone: (201) 364 1824.
Seabrook Buddhist Church, Northville Road, Seabrook, New Jersey 08302. Phone: (609) 358 3766.

USA *New Mexico*

Kagyu Shenpen Kunchab, Ervine Street, Sante Fe, New Mexico 87501.
Karma Ngawang Yonten, 368 Hillside, Sante Fe, New Mexico 87501.
Sante Fe Dharma Study Group, 951 Camino Santander, Sante Fe, New Mexico 87501. Phone: (505) 982 9675.
Sante Fe Karma Thegsum Choling, C/- B & T Thomas, 42½ E Coronado Road, Sante Fe, New Mexico 87501. Phone: (505) 982 5918.
Sante Fe Karma Thegsum Choling Retreat Centre, Box 32, Puerto De Luna, New Mexico 88432.

USA *New York*

Advaitayana Buddhism 'The Laughing Man Institute' 48 East 78th Street, New York, New York 10021.
American Buddhist & Taoist Association of NY Inc., 81 Bowery, New York, New York 10002.
American Society of Buddhist Studies, 214 Centre Street, New York, New York 10013. Phone: (212) 966 1021.
Beech Hill Pond Meditation Centre, Box 64, West Danby, New York 14896.
Buddhist Association of US, 3070 Albany Crescent, Bronx, New York 10472. Phone: (212) 884 9111.
Buddhist Church of New York, 332 Riverside Drive, New York, New York 10025. Phone: (212) 678 9214.
Buddhist Cultural Institute, 140 E 63rd St Apt 351, New York, New York 10021.
Buddhist Insight Meditation Society of New York, C/- G Cowan, 302 W 79th Street, New York, New York 10024. Phone: (212) 787 7347.

Buffalo Meditation Society, 415 Franklin Street, Buffalo, New York 14202. Phone: (716) 854 8195.

Ch'an Centre, Institute of Chung-Hwa Buddhist Culture, 90-31 Corona Avenue, Elmhurst, New York 11373. Phone: (212) 592 6593.

China Buddhist Association, 245 Canal Street, 2nd Floor, New York, New York 10012. Phone: (212) 226 9183/9434.

China Buddhist Association, Crum Elbow Road, Box 354, Hyde Park, New York 12538.

Chogye International Zen Centre of New York, 39 E 31st Street, New York, New York 10016. Phone: (212) 683 5049.

Chung Te Buddhist Association, 152 Henry Street, New York, New York 10002. Phone: (212) 577 9012.

Dai Bosatsu Zendo, Star Route, Beecher Lake, Livingston Manor, New York 12758. Phone: (914) 439 4566.

Dharmadhatu Meditation Center 231 W 20th Street, Floral Park, New York 11001. Phone: (212) 989 4792.

Dharmadhatu Meditation Centre, 49 E Street, New York, New York 10010. Phone: (212) 673 7340.

Dharmapala Inc., 32 East 32nd Street, New York, New York 10016. Phone: (212) 683 5247.

Eastern Buddhist Association, 9 Chatham Square, 2nd Floor, New York, New York 10038. Phone: (212) 577 9741.

Eastern States Buddhist Temple of America, 64 Mott Street, New York, New York 10013. Phone: (212) 226 9770.

First Zen Institute of America, 113 E 30th Street, New York, New York 10016. Phone: (212) 684 9487.

Gangjong Namgyal, Star Route, Livingston Manor, New York 12758. Phone: (212) 684 9487.

Horin Buddhist Centre, 28 E 35th Street, 3rd Floor, New York, New York 10016. Phone: (212) 784 3647.

International Dai Botsu Zendo, 223 East 67th Street, New York, New York 10021.

Ithaca Karma Thegsum Choling, 310 North Geneva Street, Ithaca, New York 14850.

Jampal Cho Ling, C/- N Clark, Apt. 1, 343 Bleecker Street, New York City, New York 11114.

Kagyu Dzamling Kunchab, 35 W 19th Street, 5th Floor, New York, New York 10011. Phone: (212) 989 5989.

Kagyu Thubten Choling, PO Box 112, New Hamburg, New York 12560. Phone: (914) 297 2500.

Kagyu Trungpa Dharma Study Group, 607 Gayuga Street, Ithaca, New York 14850. Phone: (607) 272 7267.

Karma Thegsum Choling, 40 S Main Avenue Apt 4S, Albany, New York 12208.

Karma Triyana Dharmachakra, 637 Washington Avenue, Albany, New York 12208. Phone: (518) 489 2151.

Karma Triyana Dharmachakra, 498 West End Avenue, Apt 1c, New York, New York 10024. Phone: (212) 580 9282.

Karma Triyana Dharmadhatu Bodhi Field, Birchwood Avenue, E Setauket, New York 11733.

Katonah Karma Thegsum Choling, Box 135, Cross River, New York 10518. Phone: (914) 763 5841.

Khmer Buddhist Society, 39 E 31st Street, New York, New York 10016. Phone: (212) 683 5049.

Korea Sung Bulsa Temple of New York, 105 E 16th Street, Apt 2N, New York, New York 10003.

A. Ling Cod Order of the Adoration, C/- Hubbell, 3 Lockwood Lane, Orchard Park, New York 14127.

Long Island Buddhist Association, 76 Miller Avenue, N Babylon, New York 11703.

Mahayana Temple, Ira Vail Road, South Cairo, New York 18482. Phone: (518) 622 9601.

Mahayana Temple, Gay Head Route, Leeds, New York 12451.

Mandala-Ji, 27 Grove Street, New York, New York 10014. Phone: (212) 989 2078.

Mongolian Foundation, 101 70 Nicholas Avenue, Corona, Queens, New York 11368.

New York Dharmadhatu, 49 East 21 Street, New York, New York 10010. Phone: (212) 673 7340.

New York Friends of Buddhism, 6 Black Alder Road, Shokan, New York 12481.

Orgyen Cho Dzong, 19W 16th Street, New York, New York 10011.

Orgyen Cho Dzong, RD 1 Box 1682, Greenville, New York 12803. Phone: (518) 966 4228.

Ploughkeepsie Dharma Study Group, C/- L & N Eddy, 550 Dutch Gardens Apt, Ploughkeepsie, New York 12601.

Sherab-Ling, Palpung Foundation, 75 Leonard Street, New York 10013.

Syracuse Dharma Study Group, 113 Stephen Place, North Syracuse, New York 13212. Phone: (315) 458 3962.

The Tibet Centre, 229E 12th Street, New York, New York 10003. Phone: (212) 684 8245.

Tibetan Buddhist Association of USA, 3070 Albany Crescent, Bronx, New York 10463.

Vajiradhammapadip Temple, 141 W 179 St, Bronx, New York. Phone: (212) 731 3307.

Warwick Karma Thegsum Choling, 13 West Street, Warwick, New York 10990. Phone: (914) 986 1060.

Young Men's Buddhist Association, 2611 Davidson Avenue, Bronx, New York, 10468. Phone: (212) 584 0621.

Yuan Tong Buddhist Temple, 45 East Broadway, 3rd Floor, New York, New York 10002. Phone: (212) 732 5059.

Zen Centre of New York, 440 West End Avenue, New York, New York 10024. Phone: (212) 724 4172.

Zen Institute, 113 East 30th Street, New York, New York,

USA *Ohio*

Columbus Dharma Study Group, 122 N Stanwood Road, Columbus, Ohio 43227. Phone: (614) 231 2540.

Dharmadhatu Athens, 20 E State Street, Athens, Ohio 47501.

Forming Karma Thegsum Choling, J Hughes, OC MR 1675, Oberlin, Ohio 43214.

Yellow Springs Zen Group, Rt 1 Box 267, Yellow Springs, Ohio 45387.

USA *Oregon*

Ashland Yeshi Nyingpo, PO Box 124, Ashland, Oregon 97520.

Dennis Ferman, 18185 NW West Union Road, Portland, Oregon 97229. Phone: (503) 645 0734.

Dorje Ling, 1517 SW Columbia, Portland, Oregon 97201.

Eugene Dharma Study Group, 1436E 22nd Street, Eugene, Oregon 97403. Phone: (503) 343 5569.

Kagyu Jangchub Choling, 1517 SW Carolina, Portland, Oregon 97298.

Karma Palden Zangmo, 4829 Biddle Road, Medford, Oregon 97502.

Newport Yeshe Nyingpo, C/- Demetra George, Box 405, Waldport, Oregon 97594. Phone: (503) 563 2817.

Oregon Buddhist Church, 3720 SE 34th Avenue, Portland, Oregon 97202. Phone: (503) 234 9456.

Orgyen Shedrip Choling, 1240 E 23rd Street, Eugene, Oregon 97403. Phone: (503) 683 3534.

Portland Dharma Study Group, 1004 SE Malden, Portland, Oregon 97202. Phone: (503) 231 8906.

Portland Yeshe Nyingpo, C/- Nancy Wangmo McGee, PO Box 15189, Portland, Oregon 97214. Phone: (503) 232 4021.

Rigpa, 6016 Westside Road, Cave Junction, Oregon 97523. Phone: (503) 592 3485.

Yeshe Nyingpo, 198 N River Road, Cottage Grove, Oregon 97424. Phone: (503) 942 7270.

USA *Pennsylvania*

Philadelphia Dharmadhatu, 2020 Sansom Street, Philadelphia, Pennsylvania 19103. Phone: (215) 925 5126.
Pittsburg Dharma Study Group, 432 Trenton Avenue, Pittsburg, Pennsylvania 15221. Phone: (412) 731 1230.
Vajradhatu Seminary, Bedford Springs, Pennsylvania.

USA *Rhode Island*

Kwan UM Zen School, 528 Pound Road, Cumberland, Rhode Island 02864. Phone: (401) 769 6476.
New England Buddhist Temple, 177 Bellevue Avenue, Providence, Rhode Island 02907. Phone: (401) 751 8768.
Providence Dharma Study Group, 104 John Street, Providence, Rhode Island 02906. Phone: (401) 751 6625.
Wat Dhammi Karma, 126 Hanover Street, Providence, Rhode Island 02907.

USA *South Carolina*

Dharmadhatu Columbia, 406 Hemphil Street, Columbia, South Carolina 29205. Phone: (803) 782 0204.

USA *Tennessee*

Buddhist Temple, 230 Treutland Street, Nashville. Tennessee 37202. Phone: (615) 254 6108.

USA *Texas*

Abilene Dharma Study Group, 2400 Arrowhead Apt 218, Abilene, Texas 79606. Phone: (915) 695 3667.
Austin Dharmadhatu, 1702 S 5th Street, Austin, Texas 78704. Phone: (512) 443 3263.
Dallas Dharma Study Group, 5545 Willis Street, Dallas, Texas 75219. Phone: (214) 821 1414.
Dharmadhatu Centre, 5439 Del Monte Drive, Houston, Texas 77027.
Dharmadhatu San Antonio, 114 Alexander Hamilton Drive, San Antonio, Texas 78228.
Dharmadhatu Texas, 806 Baylor Street, Austin Texas 78703.
Dharma Study Group, C/- S Luna, 106 Cyril Drive, San Antonio, Texas 78218.
Houston Dharma Study Group, 1901 Lexington, Houston, Texas 77098. Phone: (713) 524 2637.
Houston Dharma Study Group, C/- D Kahn, 16803 Imperial Valley, Dr 174 Houston, Texas 77060.
Texas Buddhist Association, 13210 Land Road, Houston, Texas 77041.

USA *Utah*

Dharma Study Group, C/- S Heins, 710 McClellan, Salt Lake City, Utah 84102.
Harold Stiles, 125 Park View Circle, Park City, Utah 84060. Phone: (801) 649 9765.
Honeyville Buddhist Church, Rt 1, Honeyville, Utah 84314. Phone: (801) 279 8477.
Salt Lake City Buddhst Church, 211 W 15th Street, Salt Lake City, Utah 84106. Phone: (801) 363 4742.

Salt Lake City Dharma Study Group, 1167 E 200th Street, Salt Lake City, Utah 84102.
Utah-Idaho Buddhist Temple, 155 North Street, Ogden, Utah 84404. Phone: (801) 392 7132.
Wat Dhammagunaram of Utah, 3417 Van Buren Avenue, Ogden, Utah 84403. Phone: (801) 621 8600.

USA *Vermont*

Burlington Dharmadhatu, 31 Elmwood Avenue, Burlington, Vermont 05401. Phone: (802) 658 6795.
Kagyu Shedrup Choling, C/- Wehage Road 1, Bristol, Vermont 05443.

USA *Virginia*

Buddhist Fellowship of Washington, C/- K Nakamura, 6622 Bestwicke Road, Burke, Virginia 22015. Phone: (703) 455 4512.
Dharma Self-Help & Analytical Centre, Rt 1, Box 283, Shipman, Virginia 22097.
Friends of Buddhism Inc., 306 Caroline Street, Fredericksburg, Virginia 22401.
Lao Buddhist Society Inc., 6925 Highland Street, Springfield, Virginia 22150.
Nam Tuyen Pagoda, 7237 Lee Highway, Falls Church, Virginia 22046. Phone: (703) 241 2284.
Washington DC Sangha, C/- Rev S Honda, 5929 Arlington Blvd, Arlington, Virginia 22203. Phone: (703) 527 0744.
Washington Sangha, 1301 S Scott Street, Arlington, Virginia 22204.

USA *Washington*

Bellingham Dharma Study Group, PO Box 2163, Bellingham, Washington 98227. Phone: (206) 676 0315.
Bo Hyon SA, 215 East 72nd Street, Tacoma, Washington 98404.
Dezhung Tulku Rinpoche, 6202 26th Avenue NE, Seattle, Washington 98115.
Dharmadhatu, 7109 Woodlawn, Seattle, Washingon 98115.
Dharmadhatu Vashon Is, Rt 1 Box 299, Vashon, Washington 98013.
Dharma Study Group, C/- J Berton, 16 Civic Circle, Bellingham, Washington 98225.
Evergreen Zen Circle, PO Box 5792, Lynwood, Washington 98036.
Karma Nordup Dorje, 9621 Seeley, Tacoma, Washington 98499.
Peter Martin, 1156 N 78th Street, Seattle, Washington 98103. Phone: (206) 523 2967.
Nihonzan Myohoji, C/- Ground Zero 16159, Clear Creek Road NW Poulsbo, Washington 98370.
Oshin, 2322 E Aloha, Seattle, Washington 98122.
Rigpa, C/- Debbie Roland. 5023 44th Avenue NE, Seattle, Washington 98015. Phone: (206) 522 2615.
Rimay Shedrub Ling, Olympic Lodge, Box 10 (Orcas Island), Deer Harbor, Washington 98243.
Sakya Tegchen Choling, 5042 18th Avenue NE, Seattle, Washington 98105. Phone: (206) 522 6967.
Sakya Tegchen Choling Center, 6555 28th Avenue NE, Seattle, Washington 98115. Phone: (206) 524 5036.
Seattle Dharma Centre, 1147 NW 57th Street, Seattle, Washington 98107. Phone: (206) 783 8484.
Seattle Karma Thegsum Choling, C/- R Baldwin. 939 25th Avenue South, Seattle, Washington 98144. Phone: (206) 325 4834.

Spokane Buddhist Church, S 927 Perry Street, Spokane, Washington 99202. Phone: (509) 534 7623.

Tacoma Buddhist Church, 1717 S Fawcett Avenue, Tacoma, Washington 98402. Phone: (206) 627 1417.

Tusum Ling, Route 1, PO Box 299, Burton, Washington 98013.

Wat Thai Washington, Federal Way, Washington, Washington State.

White River Buddhist Church, 3625 Auburn Way N Auburn, Washington 98002. Phone: (206) 833 1442.

Yakima Buddhist Church, 212 W 2nd Street, Wanato, Washington 98951. Phone: (509) 877 2743.

Zen Centre, 1517 34th Apt, Seattle, Washington 98112.

USA *Washington DC*

Buddhist Congregational Church of America, 5333 or 5401 16th St NW, Washington DC 20011. Phone: (202) 329 2423.

Buddhist Vihara Society Inc, 5017 16th St NW, Washington DC 20011. Phone: (202) 723 0773.

Buddhist Women of North America, 825 New Hampshire Avenue NW, Washington DC 20037.

Dharmadhatu Washingon, 3229 Idaho Avenue NW, Washington DC 20016.

Drikung Dharma Centre, 3454 Macomb Street, Washington DC 20008.

Drikung Kagyu Dharma Center, 5307 Conn Avenue NW, Washington DC 20015.

Nihhonzan Myohoji Inc, 4900 16th Street NW, Washington DC 20011. Phone: (202) 291 2047.

Vietnamese American Buddhist Association, 7060 Wyndale Street, NW, Washington DC 20015. Phone: (202) 966 0015.

Washington Buddhist Vihara, 5017 16th Street NW, Washington DC.

Washington DC Dharmadhatu, 1424 Wisconsin Avenue NW, Washington DC. Phone: (202) 338 7090.

Washington Group Downtown Zendo, 1717 P Street NW, Washington DC 20036. Phone: (202) 234 4102.

Zen Buddhist Centre of Washington, 500 Butternut Street NW, Washington DC 20012. Phone: (202) 829 1966.

USA *Wisconsin*

Buddhist Centre of Milwaukee, C/- R Bogan, PO Box 4165, Milwaukee, Wisconsin 53210.

Eau Claire Dharma Study Group, (Prof R Gross), 126 Gilbert Avenue, Eau Claire, Wisconsin 54701. Phone: (715) 834 9612.

Ganden Mahayana Centre, 4548 Schneider Road, Oregon, Wisconsin 53575. Phone: (608) 835 5572.

Mada Bohi Society, PO Box 10165, Milwaukee, Wisconsin 53210. Madison Zen Group, 1820 Jefferson Street, Madison, Wisconsin 53711.

USSR

Central Religious Board of Buddhist Organisations of the USSR, Buryat Autonomous.

Central Religious Buddhist Organisation of the USSR, A-167 Theatre Alley 2, Moscow City 125167.

Datsan Monastery, Settlement Aginskol, Buriyat Autonomous.

Invorginski Datsan Monastery, Settlement Ivorga, Buriyat Autonomous.

VENEZUELA

Caracas Karma Thegsum Choling, Apartado 2775, Carmelitas, Caracas.

VIETNAM

Co Le Pagoda, Nam Ninh District, 14A Nam Quinh.
Theravadin Buddhist Association, Sukha Vihara, 491/132 Phan Dinh Phing, Ho Chi Minh City.
Unified Buddhist Congregation, An-Quang Pagoda, 243 Su Van Street, Ho Chi Minh City.
United Buddhist Association of Vietnam, 74 Quan Su, Hanoi.
United Vietnam Buddhist Association, 716 Vo Di Nquy Phu Nhuan, Ho Chi Minh City.

Wisdom Publications, London, are publishers of Buddhist books, posters, prints, card, prayers, and audio & video tapes. Send for our **52-page catalogue,** to either our **London office,** Wisdom Publications, 23 Dering Street, London W1, England, phone (01) 499 0925, or to any of our **distributors worldwide.**
Australia Wisdom Publications, PO Box 1326, Chatswood, NSW 2067, phone (02) 909 1330. **Benelux** Maitreya Distributors, Raadhuisdjik 9, 6627 AC Maasbommel, Holland, phone (08876) 2188. **Hong Kong** Wisdom Publications, PO Box 98650, Tsimshatsui, phone (3) 721 1974. **India** Tushita Mahayana Meditation Centre, 5/5 Shantiniketan, New Delhi 110021, phone 67 54 68. **Italy** Chiara Luce Edizioni, Istituto Lama Tzong Khapa, 56040 Pomaia, phone (050) 68976. **Japan** Tibet Culture Centre, Room 401 Gotanda Lilas Hi-Town, 15-12-2 Nishi Gotanda, Shinagawa-Ku, Tokyo 141, phone (03) 490 7868. **Nepal** Himalayan Yogic Institute, PO Box 817, Kathmandu. **Singapore** Buddhist Wisdom Circulation Services, Apt Blk 79, Marine Drive 17-26, Singapore 1544, phone 348 4776. **Spain** Publicaciones Dharma, Apartado 218, Novelda (Alicante). **Switzerland** Dechen Ling, PO Box 36, 8344 Baretswil, phone (01) 939 16 51. **UK** Element Books, Longmead, Shaftesbury, Dorset, phone (0747) 51339. **USA** Wisdom Publications, Robyn Brentano, PO Box 62, Prince Street Station, New York, NY 10012, phone (212) 677 3377. The Great Tradition, 750 Adrian Way, Suite 111, San Rafael, Ca 94903, phone (415) 492 9382. Snow Lion Publications, PO Box 6483, Itacha, NY 14850, phone (607) 273 8506. **West Germany** Diamant Verlag, Jägerndorf 1½, 8382 Arnstorf, phone (08723) 2396.

Some Wisdom books

We publish our Buddhist theory-and-practice titles in three broad categories:
> Basic Books: Orange Series
> Intermediate Books: White Series
> Advanced Books: Blue Series

These categories indicate the general level of approach of each title, whether sutra or tantra, and thus are a practical guide for readers in their choice of the most appropriate books.

How to Meditate
Kathleen McDonald
A practical guide
Edited by Robina Courtin

What is meditation? Why practise it? Which technique is best for me? How do I do it? The answers to these often-asked questions are contained in this down-to-earth book written and compiled by a Western Buddhist nun with solid experience in both the practice and teaching of meditation.

How to Meditate contains a wealth of practical advice on a variety of authentic and proven techniques: simple breathing and mindfulness exercises, meditation on emptiness, meditations using visualization and mantra, analytical meditations on death and suffering, meditations utilizing the psychic channels – the whole spectrum of techniques used by Tibetan Buddhists is covered. Also included are many of the simple prayers associated with Mahayana practice.

This book is written specifically for people wanting to practise meditation, but is ideal also for anyone who simply wants to know what meditation is all about.

216pp, illustrations, 0 86171 009 6
£4.95/$9.95

A Wisdon Basic Book · Orange Series

Opening the Eye of New Awareness
The Dalai Lama
Translated by Donald S. Lopez, with Jeffrey Hopkins

In the preface to this book, written four years after his exile
from Tibet, the Dalai Lama says that he intended it "for
those who do not have the leisure to study the great texts,
profound and full of impact."

Opening the Eye of New Awareness is a succinct yet
thorough presentation of the doctrines of Buddhism as they
were studied and practised for a thousand years in Tibet.
The Dalai Lama begins with a discussion of the need for
religious practice and an explanation of the proofs for the
existence of rebirth. He explains ultimate and conventional
truths; the trainings in ethics, meditative stabilization and
wisdom; the practice of the path in the Lesser, Perfection
and Secret Mantra, or Tantra, Vehicles; and the nature of
Buddhahood. He concludes with a brief history of Tibetan
Buddhism that clearly shows the continuity between late
Indian Mahayana Buddhism and the Buddhism of Tibet,
dispelling the idea that Tibetan Buddhism is "Lamaism"
and unrelated to the central currents of Buddhist thought.

Opening the Eye of New Awareness is the only text of the
Dalai Lama outlining the entire path to be published in a
Western language. It is an invaluable handbook for the
study of Buddhism both in colleges and by the individual

130pp, 0 86171 036 3

A Wisdom Intermediate Book · White Series

First in the new series of Wisdom Tibet Books

In Exile from the Land of Snows
John F. Avedon
The first full account of the Dalai Lama and Tibet
since the Chinese conquest.

For over 2,000 years, Tibet held itself aloof from the affairs
of the world. Perched at 15,000 feet, in the shadow of the
Himalayas, it was a feudal kingdom of peasants, Buddhist
monks and nuns, nomads and aristocrats, whose temporal
and spiritual leader was the Dalai Lama. *In Exile from the
Land of Snows* gives us, for the first time, a complete and
graphic account of how this tranquil, isolated nation was
wrenched into the nightmares of the twentieth century and
how her patient, gentle and courageous people have
resisted their fate.

The story begins in 1950, when Tibet is invaded by the
newly triumphant People's Liberation Army of Communist
China. Routing the meagre Tibetan forces in three weeks,
the Chinese compel the Dalai Lama, just turned sixteen, to
administer a puppet government under their tutelage.
"Democratic reforms" follow that strip the inhabitants of
their land, their property and all other human rights.
Revolt is inevitable, and, in 1959, following a massive
uprising in Lhasa, the capital, the Dalai Lama is forced to
seek refuge in India.

What happens next is completely unexpected. The Dalai
Lama and the 100,000 exiles who eventually join him do
more than survive; they flourish, giving new life to their
unique heritage and holding fast to their dreams of a free
and independent Tibet. Working feverishly, they scratch
farms out of the jungle, build libraries and monasteries,
create an independent school system and establish a
democratic government-in-exile.

John F. Avedon tells us the story in terms of its central
people: a young man who was a destitute refugee at the age
of ten and who has since risen to the highest circles of exile
governement; another who was trained by the CIA (in
Colorado) to wage guerrilla war against the Chinese; the

State Oracle, whose gifts of prophecy and vision are consulted on all matters of policy; a doctor of Tibetan medicine who has helped preserve the ancient teachings of his extraordinary science; and, most revealingly, the son of peasants, the Dalai Lama himself, whose birth and destiny were foreseen, the compassionate overseer of all their efforts.

Those they struggle for – the millions who have remained in Tibet – have endured torture, imprisonment forced labour brigades, brutal "re-education" classes, famine and the hysteria of the Cultural Revolution. They have seen their religion desecrated and their land transformed into a fortress state studded with military installations, including China's largest nuclear missile base. And we are witness to their story as well – through the accounts of the Dalai Lama's personal physican (who was punished for his "crimes" by twenty-one years in Chinese prison camps) and those of the Tibetan representatives Peking has allowed to visit their homeland since the death of Mao and the purge of the Gang of Four.

Despite all their efforts, the Chinese have failed to subdue the Tibetans, and, as this book amply documents, they know it, thus, in 1978, they began to make overtures to the Dalai Lama, gestures that have led to negotiations for his possible return.

Most of the material in this book – the triumphs of the exiles, the devastation wrought by the Chinese, the inner workings of Tibetan Buddhism – has never before been made known. Certainly no other writer has been closer to this unique story, a story filled with tragedy, but suffused with a rare sense of resilience and hope.

480pp, 60 black & white and colour photos, 0 86171 029 0

A Wisdom Tibet Book